RECLAIMING YOUR DESTINY

SIX ESSENTIAL KEYS TO **PERSONAL FREEDOM**

Kathy—
"And you will
you know the
truth and the
truth will set
you free." John
8:32

Connie
Ioset
9-18-22

CONNIE L. IOSET

A Six Week Bible Study in Living Without Regrets

RECLAIMING YOUR DESTINY

ISBN (Print Edition): 978-1-66784-062-8

Printed in the United States of America

Published by Connie L. Ioset, atthehemofthegarment@gmail.com

Design by BookBaby

Portions of text quoted from Living Without Regrets 6 Essential Keys to Personal Freedom
with permission by Cinda M. Gregory © 2019

Dedication

This book is dedicated to my dear friend, Cinda Gregory. Cinda, you continually stretched me and taught me how to step out of my comfort zone. Through your teachings on freedom, I was set free. Through the opportunities to minister alongside you and Bob, I encountered the power of the Holy Spirit to heal not only me but others as well. Your transparency and vulnerability touched my life in so many ways, giving me permission to take a risk and to start believing in myself. It was your sensitivity to the Holy Spirit that brought truth and freedom to my life. Like you, I have become passionate about helping others find freedom through the Father. This Bible Study would never have been written had it not been for your ability to see something in me that I could never see. This has been one of the greatest challenges that I have ever accepted, and without God, this would have never been written. Thank you for this lifechanging opportunity.

I am forever grateful for your love, friendship, and willingness to walk alongside me over these past twenty-three years and be my mentor. Thank you for pouring into me and fueling my passion for God's Word and the freedom it brings. I will forever miss you, but someday we will be reunited.

Acknowledgements

There are so many people that have encouraged me along this journey. It would have never been completed without the help of so many dedicated people that walked beside me.

Thank you to my brother-in-law, Dr. Mark Ioset, for being my primary editor. Mark, I could not have done this without you. Your expertise of the English language and your Biblical knowledge was so helpful in editing the manuscript. Sue Kablack, your keen eye for detail was exactly what I needed to bring this book to completion. Harold Coleman, your technology skills brought us across the finish line. Thank you.

Wendy Chapura, you rose to the challenge of being the first person to volunteer to take the study. I am so grateful that you were willing to invest all the time you put into working through the study, not once but twice! Your feedback was invaluable, and I am forever grateful to you for being my willing participant.

To my husband Scot, thank you for believing in me and encouraging me every step of the way. Your love and patience allowed me to finish this race put before me. You carried me across the finish line. Thank you.

Brittany, Benjamin, and Samuel, thank you for all you have taught me over the years of being your mom. So many times, you have shown me the Father's heart through the things you have said and done. Thank you for giving me permission to use you in this study and giving me your input. I am forever grateful to the Father for blessing me with three such amazing children.

To my mother, Doris Hanes, thank you for teaching me to love God's Word through your example as I was growing up. Your passion for Bible Study has impacted my life in so many ways and has taught me that there is no greater time spent than that with the Lord.

Lastly, but most importantly, thank you to my Heavenly Father. You began preparing me way before Cinda ever asked me to write this study. You made me passionate about reading scripture. You taught me the art of meditating on Scripture and showed me how exciting and challenging Scripture is. Thank you for guiding me every step of the way. You are the one who authored every page I wrote. You taught me anything is possible. I never thought I could write this study. You already knew I could – thank you precious Daddy.

Table of Contents

Preface

My husband and I were two of the lucky ones to sit under Cinda and Bob Gregory's leadership. I remember clearly the first time I met Cinda. My husband, Scot, and I had just come out of a very traumatic situation and had left a church that we loved. We then spent several painful months looking for a new church. We knew that God had a place for us, we just had not found it yet. But then we walked into Randallsville Baptist Church (now Randallsville New Life Church) in Hamilton, New York. The minute we walked in the door, we knew that God was calling us to make this our church home. We had not heard a worship song, listened to a prayer, or even talked to anyone; we just knew in our Spirit. This was home.

A few weeks after we began attending church there, I slipped on my icy driveway and severely injured my arm. I will not go into the details of that whole incident but suffice it to say that I was in severe pain, my hand was turning purple and numb, and the doctor was concerned about irreversible nerve damage that could cause immobility in my arm and hand. I thought I had broken my elbow, but the doctor's diagnosis was much more disturbing.

We headed to church the next week after my fall with my arm in a sling, and I was in such pain that I was nauseated. As the worship music began, I found myself sitting down holding my arm. I wanted to leave. I was miserable, but for **"some"** reason we did not. When the service ended, I beelined toward the door, but I did not make it there before a beautiful young lady, Cinda, came up to me and said, "Don't leave until you have Harry pray for you." I asked her, "Who is Harry?" I did not know this person, but Cinda was adamant that I stay, so I said, "Okay". After all, I certainly believed in the power of prayer, so what did I have to lose? Cinda quickly introduced me to Harry and his wife, Fern. They took me up to the front of the church by the communion table. Harry did not ask me about my injury or what had happened. He just spoke to me and explained that often when He prayed his hand would begin to tremble and that was just the Holy Spirit moving. So, Harry, Fern, Cinda and I began to pray. I must admit, my mind was more focused on the pain than the prayer, UNTIL Harry stopped at my shoulder and his hand began to tremble. He told me that I had a fracture in my shoulder. I looked up at him and said, "No it is my elbow." He continued to pray and said, "No, the Lord is telling me you have a fracture in your shoulder," and he began to pray. As he prayed, I remember feeling a burning like fire in my shoulder, and I instantly became so nauseated that I thought I was going to throw up. I looked to Cinda and said, "I think I am going to throw up." They grabbed a trash can, but I was thankful I did not need to use it after all. I left the church knowing that God was healing my shoulder. He not only healed it, but that afternoon I painted my son's room using that arm! Praise Jesus! He is the healer!

I later learned from Cinda an interesting fact. That Sunday was Harry and Fern's 50th wedding anniversary, and they were planning on leaving church early to attend an anniversary celebration their family had planned for them. But at the beginning of the service God pointed me out to Harry and said, "You aren't leaving; you have to stay and pray for that lady." So, Harry was obedient. He stayed. He prayed. God healed. Both Cinda and Harry heard the voice of God, and in their obedience, I was healed.

From that time forward Cinda and I became friends. She was someone I wanted to be like. She was so bubbly, her smile brightened up the room, and she laughed a lot. I never laughed much, but when I was around Cinda I found myself laughing, sometimes so hard my sides hurt. I admired how she embraced ministry. Before I knew it, Cinda invited Scot and I to attend a Marriage Ministries Group that they were leading at their house. We immediately agreed. I thought it would be "fun" to learn from Bob and Cinda, so we began the course. It was not long before I realized that the course was not at all what I thought it would be. It was challenging the foundation of our marriage, and things were becoming uncomfortable. The course work, and Cinda and Bob's discernment from the Holy Spirit, spoke into those deep hidden places of our heart. It was not long before Bob was confronting Scot in the hallway at church, and I was beginning to feel like I needed to run away from this course. We stuck with it, mostly because we did not want to offend our newfound friends. Through Cinda and Bob's own vulnerability and transparency in talking about the trials in their marriage, Scot and I experienced a new freedom and healing in our marriage. It changed our lives. I was so grateful for how the Holy Spirit moved so powerfully through them to bring freedom to us. That was their heart. It quickly became my heart.

I took this newfound freedom and began leading an Interdenominational Bible Study at a church in the Village of Hamilton. Having been an Army wife for eleven years, I had experienced the beauty of being a part of many different denominations in the Body of Christ. Every church was like a different flavor of ice cream. They were special and unique in some ways, but the foundation was the same.

There was one church, Severens Valley Baptist Church in Elizabethtown, Kentucky, that impacted our world forever. We signed up for a Sunday School class that was doing a study by Henry Blackaby called "Experiencing God: Knowing and Doing the Will of God." It was in this study my husband came to hear the voice of God. While driving fast down a country road and coming into a blind curve, he heard a voice command, "Stop this car now!" He pulled over, and a drunk driver, who was going way too fast, came around the corner in our lane passing another car. If we had not pulled over, we probably would have died or been severely injured. You could say we "experienced God" that night because my husband accepted Jesus as Lord of his life on the spot. The reality that God

speaks to His children was cemented in our hearts and forever changed our walk with the Lord. It was through this Bible Study that I discovered the importance of studying God's Word.

Shortly after taking that course, Scot and I attended an Emmaus Walk. On this weekend, we experienced the "love" of God in a way that totally overwhelmed us and propelled us into a whole new love for the Body of Christ and how God uses them to show His all-encompassing love for us. The love showered on us that weekend, gave us a glimpse of the love of the Father that we had never experienced before. Neither one of us wanted to leave the weekend. We were changed forever.

With this newfound experience of learning to hear the voice of God, experiencing the lavish love of God for us, and studying the word of God, we were beginning to change from head knowledge to heart knowledge. There was still a lot to learn, and God challenged us constantly in our walks, calling us to embrace the refiner's fire in our lives.

Studying God's Word was planted in me as a child from watching my mom. Every night after dinner and the dishes were done, she would go sit in the green velvet chair in the living room and open up her Bible and study. Night after night, year after year I watched her. It was what she taught me by her actions that stuck with me. God's Word was important. As a teenager I did not really think much about it, but as I grew up and started living life on my own, that vision of her in her green chair stuck with me. And then it happened; studying God's Word became my own passion. It did not happen overnight. It was through years of walking through life that I realized how desperately I needed Him to be real and active in my life. The Word tells us "If we seek Him, we will find Him." This is true. When you honestly put your heart toward seeking Him, He is more than happy to let you find Him. He is not hiding, He is waiting. Bible Study has become a major passion in my life. I have led women's Bible study for thirty years. I love the fact that in my current Bible Study, ladies from over thirty different churches have come together in our village to study the Word of God.

I have always had a heart to see the broken-hearted healed, the prisoner set free, the sick healed. I had witnessed several miracles in my life, and I knew that God works through his children to bring healing to this earth. I wanted Him to use me that way, but my own insecurity in stepping into the unknown prevented me from stepping out, until Cinda. Cinda had a way of pushing me into situations that were uncomfortable for me. She did not force me, but her words, love and encouragement always convinced me to say "yes" to the very thing that terrified me. The desire to step out in ministry was such a yearning in my heart, yet my heart was imprisoned in walls of insecurity, self-condemnation, fear and doubt. God could never use me. Cinda asked me to become a part of their ministry team for Marriage Ministries International. The thought of leading a small group into the presence of the Holy Spirit so that He would come and bring healing to people in my group was terrifying! What if the Holy Spirit did not show? What if I did not hear His voice or discern anything? As long as I had this fear and pressure on myself that I had to do something, nothing happened. But as I surrendered myself under the Holy Spirit, He began to speak to me and heal others. He always shows up for His children because He loves them. I will forever be thankful to Cinda and Bob for the way they always looked at the potential in others. These seminars were a great training ground for me and built my confidence. It taught me that if I simply facilitate what God is already doing, miraculous things will happen! It is all about Him. We are just the "hands" He chooses to use.

After Cinda published her book, <u>Living Without Regrets – Six Essential Keys to Personal Freedom</u>, there was a large response from people asking for a Bible Study to accompany the book. Cinda asked me to write the study. Once again, Cinda was challenging me in areas of my life I never thought nor dreamed of being challenged. Cinda's ability to discern the Holy Spirit has been uncanny. When she asked me about writing this study, I immediately knew it was God because He had already been preparing me without my knowing it. I embarked on this new adventure with the Father, completely relying on His guidance and voice to lead me. Without Him I had nothing, but with Him, He had much to say about your freedom. This study is meant to be done alongside Cinda Gregory's book, <u>Living Without Regrets: Six Essential Keys to Freedom</u>; however, it can also stand alone. Throughout the book I will refer to much of Cinda's writings, but I will refer to her quotes simply by saying, "Cinda wrote…" in the book and her quote will follow.

Cinda's walk through ovarian cancer has been a faith journey for me. I have watched how she and Bob have been surrounded with people that have laid down their lives in so many ways to minister to them. They are reaping the harvest that they have sown into others. God has used Bob and Cinda to bring freedom to so many lives, and in return, those brothers and sisters in Christ are bringing life to her. When I think of Cinda, I think of the caterpillar that has been encased in the chrysalis. Cinda has been encased by the Body of Christ. She is hemmed in with their love, prayers and sacrifices. God is working inside the chrysalis, bringing new life, a creation that is unrecognizable from the one that was before. Cinda has walked in the fire; she has learned the keys to living life without regrets. Her book is a recollection of her walk into freedom. These six essential keys to personal freedom are for you. It is our hope together, partnering with the Holy Spirit, that you would walk in freedom in every area of your life.

Introductory Session – Building a Solid Foundation

And so, it begins … the journey of freedom. Your freedom was meant to be from the beginning of time. Somehow through life we have given up the rights to our freedom and have allowed our lives to be imprisoned by things that were never meant to be. You have the keys in your hand to unlock your freedom. Will you put the key in the lock and turn it, so the door to freedom opens for you? This is your time … freedom is yours for the taking.

"If You See the Fruit, You Have Got the Root!"[1]

The choices you make chart the course of your life. Each decision or choice you make has consequences that will lead you into a place of freedom or bondage. In Scripture, there is a principle called sowing and reaping. Each decision and choice you make will bring forth a harvest that is either good (spiritual growth) or bad (taking you away from God).

> *"Be not deceived; God is not mocked: for whatever a man soweth, that shall he also reap. For he that soweth to his flesh, shall of the flesh reap corruption; but he that soweth to the Spirit shall of the Spirit reap life everlasting." Galatians 6:7-8 (KJV)*

> *"Do not be misled; remember that you can't ignore God and get away with it; a man will always reap just the kind of crop he sows. If he sows to please his own wrong desires, he will be planting seeds of evil and he will surely reap a harvest of spiritual decay and death; but if he plants the good things of the Spirit, he will reap the everlasting life which the holy Spirit gives him" Galatians 6:7-8 (TLB)*

When we experience the freedom that only Christ can bring, we begin to reap a good harvest. What does your harvest look like? Do you like what you are reaping in your life so far? Do you have regrets about how you have lived your life? Do you think about the past and let the "what if" scenarios run through your head? Are there dreams you wish had happened, things you could have done but didn't, and you are now wondering, "what if?"

What are the "what if's" that run through your head? Write down any "what ifs" you have or had.

Now that you have written them down, write a big X over them. It is time to stop thinking about the "what ifs" that focus on the past, things you cannot change.

The good news is that things are about to change. Start looking forward to the potential of "what is" to come. There is the smell of freedom in the air – do you smell it? Do you want it? During this study we are going to focus on the "Six Essential Keys to Personal Freedom," that Cinda Gregory writes about in her book <u>Living Without Regrets – Six Essential Keys to Personal Freedom</u>, that will help you quit living life with regrets. The Bible speaks of living life like a race. You are focused on the finish line and the prize set before you. Many people start the race well, but do not end well. We lose our focus by fixating on the things of the world and soon we are derailed, completely off course. No matter what you have been through, God can get you back on track. Regardless of your past, you can end well. So, put on your running shoes and focus your eyes on Jesus … Freedom is in the air.

God's Great Gift of Love

From the very beginning of time, God had one thing on His heart: to dwell with man. God created a beautiful garden and placed man and woman in it and dwelled with them there. They walked together, talked together, enjoyed each other's presence until man's free will chose to disobey God's word. Shortly thereafter, they found themselves banished from the garden and separated from God. From that moment, God started creating a pathway to bring man back in relationship with Himself. He spoke to Moses and told him to build a tabernacle for Him to dwell in so He could be with His people. Whenever the Israelites moved, God moved with them. King David desired to build God a permanent temple, but God told him, "No", that his son Solomon would be the one to build it. Solomon built the Lord a beautiful temple and God continued to dwell in it with man. In the book of John, the most incredible thing happened: "The Word became flesh and made his dwelling among us." (John 1:14) Jesus walked on this earth alongside man and taught the heart of the Father to all whom He came in contact. After three short years of ministry, the ultimate act of love was given:

> *"For God so loved the world that he gave his one and only Son, that whoever believes in him shall not perish but have eternal life." John 3:16 (NIV)*

Now the Holy Spirit (God) dwells within man. God chooses to live inside each of us. The Father gave His Son, Jesus, to die for us so we could dwell with Him forever. The choice to allow Jesus in our lives is up to us. If we choose to accept Jesus in our lives the most incredible thing happens, the Holy Spirit takes up residence inside of us! God now dwells in the place He has always desired to be-within you and me. And, finally, one day we will all dwell in the new Jerusalem with Him.

It is in the "dwelling" that our lives are changed forever. It is in the still, small whisper from within that the God of all creation leads us to our ultimate freedom in Him. God planned for us to lead a victorious life, full and abundant. But how do we walk in this freedom, where do we start? The first step is acknowledging our sin problem.

Sin Breaks the Relationship – God's Love Restores the Relationship

"For all have sinned and fall short of the glory of God." Romans 3:23 (NIV)

"All of us have become like one who is unclean, and our righteous acts are like filthy rags; we all shrivel up like a leaf, and like the wind our sins sweep us away." Isaiah 64:6 (NIV)

"Sin is a slippery slope, and it will eventually catch up with you. One sin leads to another, and another, like lie upon lie, and it gets easier to sin each time we do it. You cannot have peace with God when your conscience is constantly convicting you regarding your sin. Repentance is the brake pedal that stops it. No matter what you have done in this life, in mere seconds you can become righteous before God. God is waiting for you to talk to Him; His ear is bent toward you. God is waiting to hear your voice. God is waiting to forgive. Go to Him and tell Him how sorry you are for the things you did, and ask Him to forgive you, and then repent (turn away) from your sin. Your slate will be clean, and you will be washed as white as snow. What is lost can be restored. That which is broken can be repaired. If you are breathing, there is hope."[2]

Take some time to reflect and come before the Father, confessing anything that He brings to your mind. You may want to write a list or just speak to Him. Repent of your sin (past/present) and ask God to give you a new start. Receive the forgiveness He gives so freely.

Write a summary of Psalm 32:2.

David wrote Psalm 32 after his affair and marriage to Bathsheba. He had gotten a married woman pregnant and then plotted to have her husband, Uriah, killed. David's sin gave him no rest. David became restless. His peace was gone. He was dealing with guilt, shame, and remorse for what he had done. The sweet fellowship that he once had with the Lord was now broken because of his sin.

Read Psalm 32:4

Did you notice the words "Your hand was heavy upon me?" God was there with David. He never left him. David sensed the presence of God with him in the midst of his sin. God's presence was calling David back to Him, to repent. Have you been in a situation where you knew you were doing wrong, yet in the midst of it you felt God there beside you, calling you to turn away from your sin? God stirs inside of us the desire to seek His forgiveness. He is calling you to be in a right relationship with Him. God does require two things of you: to ask for forgiveness and to turn away from your sin – to repent. To repent means you are closing the door to past sin and refusing to revisit it anymore. There are times when you repent, and are determined to turn away, yet find yourself falling right back into the place of sin you were before. The enemy knows our weakness and will try to set traps for us to fall back into the sinful ways of our past. God is there for you, to help you walk out your victory. God knows your heart and your weakness, and He will walk through it with you until victory comes. When God forgives, He forgets (period!). He chooses to forget because He is more concerned with His relationship with you than with anything else. So be encouraged and see what God tells us in the following Scriptures regarding your sin when you ask for forgiveness and repent. It is good news indeed.

What do the following Scriptures say God does when we ask for forgiveness and repent of our sin?

Psalm 103:11-12

Isaiah 1:18

Acts 3:19

Hebrews 10:17

Romans 4:8

Isaiah 44:22

Micah 7:18

God makes it clear that He does not hold onto your sin. When you confess it, He is more than anxious to get rid of it. He lets it go and remembers it no more. The problem is so often we do not let it go. We continue to live our life in self-imposed bondage. When we do not let go, we develop a harvest of bad fruit which brings a whole crop of its own. God knows the danger of us not forgiving ourselves. Unforgiveness of self can lead to self-hatred, which can leave a person feeling unloved, unworthy, rejected, anxious, angry, ashamed, insecure, fearful, feelings of low self-esteem and uselessness. Therefore, it is so important to meditate on Scriptures that remind us that our sin is removed and remembered no more by God. When we believe God's truth as He speaks it through Scripture, we can once and for all embrace the gift of forgiveness and freedom that Jesus gives. If God, the Creator of the universe, thinks we are worthy of His forgiveness, then we need to accept it for ourselves and start living as forgiven people. Do not walk with your head hanging low; stand tall and let God be the lifter of your head. You are a forgiven child of God.

Spend some time in prayer sharing with God how you feel about yourself and ask him to help you see yourself as He does.

God is a giver of good gifts and wants to give you something in exchange for your sin. Fill in the blanks to complete the Scriptures.

Isaiah 61:10

"I delight greatly in the Lord; my soul rejoices in my God. For he has _____ me with _____ and arrayed me in a _____ of His _____ , as a bridegroom adorns his head like a priest, and as a bride adorns herself with her jewels." (NIV)

Isaiah 52:1

"Clothe yourself with _____ . Put on your garments of _____ ." (NIV)

Psalm 103:4

"Who redeems your life from the pit and _____ you with _____ and _____ ." (NIV)

Isaiah 62:2-3

"You will be called by a new name, that the mouth of the Lord will bestow. You will be a _____ of _____ in the Lord's hand." (NIV)

Take Time to Pray

The single most important thing you can do in your lifetime is to ask Jesus to be your personal Lord and Savior. If you have never done this, now is the time to get yourself right with God. Here is a prayer you can pray to give your life to Jesus:

Lord Jesus, I come before your throne of grace, and I realize Lord that I need you in my life. I confess to you that I am a sinner, and I need your forgiveness. Father, I ask your forgiveness for all the times in my life that I have sinned against you. I repent of my sin, and I ask that you come into my life and be my Savior. I believe that Jesus died, was buried, and rose from the dead so that I could have a relationship with you. Jesus, thank you for taking my sin upon yourself and dying for me. Come and dwell in me. Be the Lord of my life. I love you Lord. Amen.

For those of you who are already believers, are there things you have been carrying inside that you need to ask God's forgiveness for? Are there things that you have not dealt with because you are too embarrassed, frustrated or too prideful to admit?

Are there things you need to repent of that you have already asked forgiveness for, but you keep revisiting it in your mind? Jesus wants you free, so do not hold onto anything that could keep you from receiving your freedom.

The foundation has been laid. Everything in this book stands on what we just learned: God wants a relationship with you. He paid a high price, the blood of His only Son, for that relationship. The only way you can ruin that relationship is by walking away, turning your back on the only One that knows you and loves you completely. God is never going to stop pursuing a love relationship with you. When you embrace the Father, freedom awaits you. Success awaits you. Hope awaits you. Joy awaits you. Abundant life awaits you. God wants to give it to you; it is up to you to choose to receive it.

Week 1:

Freedom –
Choosing to Be Made Whole

"Heal your past; you'll redeem your future."

Key #1 – Freedom Is a Choice

Day 1:
CONVICTION VERSUS SHAME

We have all done it. We find ourselves experiencing something we dislike over and over, or we see something within us (an attitude or behavior) that we want to change. We determine that we are going to stop it. We are going to take charge and get that "thing" out of our life once and for all. We strategize, we read books, we get counsel, and we begin the battle of changing ourselves. We may even experience some success, but then we turn around and we find ourselves "once again" in the same place, doing the same thing we vowed we would never do. We are instantly thrown into the emotions of denial, shock, embarrassment, and frustration. We begin to feel powerless that we cannot even control our own emotions, feelings, and actions. We no longer feel in control of the path our life is taking. Whether you have experienced a violation you could not control, a habitual sin you cannot break, or you have made a choice that got you into a situation you never intended, you can begin to feel like you are locked in a prison with no way out. Shame, guilt, or hopelessness can come upon you in an instant declaring your imprisonment for a lifetime.

In the book, <u>Living Life Without Regrets, The Six Essential Keys to Personal Freedom</u>, Cinda described what she experienced as a young child that she called "the shroud of shame."

"A deep sense of shame filled me. It had to be my fault. The shame became a shroud that I secretly wrapped myself in. I lived under this darkness for the next twenty-five years. Was this feeling rational? No. Had anyone blamed me? Absolutely not. Yet I could not silence the voice of self-condemnation. The attack shattered my young world and robbed me of my innocence."[3]

"The shame and embarrassment cut deeply into my heart, carving out a place where I could hide and "feel safe" once again. It became my new normal. As time went on, I further separated myself from the pain, gaining so much distance from it that one day, it seemed as if it had never happened at all! It became someone else's life … unfortunately, the truth was irrefutable. It had a definite impact and forever changed my life, whether I wanted to admit it or not."[4]

Many people have experienced this shroud of shame. A cloak that once put on never seems to want to come off. That cloak is not from God, and He wants to remove it. God's heart is all about healing and saving. God wants you whole, but there is a counter part that does not, the enemy of your soul. Satan wants you to be confused by taking the Holy Spirit's conviction and turning it into shame. It is critical for one to know the difference between conviction and shame.

"To Convict means: to expose, lay bare, to detect, to reveal your mistake to you. The feeling of conviction urges you to make something right, and when you repent, it is gone. Conviction is good and says: "What you did was wrong." Conviction is meant to be uncomfortable so that we quickly seek repentance and find relief and restoration in God. Apologize quickly and do not do it again. The Holy Spirit convicts our hearts, and as a result it will shape you into a better person."[5]

"Shame means: to humiliate, dishonor, and to disgrace. Fear and shame are tools of the enemy. They are like bullies, and they will not leave without a fight, yet when you decide to face them, they will flee. Shame is evil and says: "You are what is wrong. You are no good, and you will never be any good. Look at what you did. You will never stop doing this. Why don't you just quit? The purpose is to get you to give up trying and to drown you in defeat. Shame will spiritually paralyze you and make you ineffective."[6] Shame often leads to you feeling guilty, dirty, or dishonored, disgraced and humiliated. This is the work of Satan and his demons. Fear and shame are some of their favorite tools to use against God's children.

In your own words write down the difference between conviction and shame:

Conviction is:

Shame is:

Are there areas in your life where the Holy Spirit is trying to show you something that you need to repent of or change? Instead of receiving conviction and repentance, you began to blame yourself and allow shame to cover you. Ask God to show you any instances in your life where the Holy Spirit

was trying to open your eyes to an area that you needed to repent of or change and you immediately began condemning yourself.

This chapter is all about freedom. To be totally free we need to seek the Father to show us the truth of our situation.

Ask Him to reveal any sinful stronghold and lies that you need to break free of in your life through the conviction of the Holy Spirit. When the Holy Spirit shows you something, then confess it to God, repent, ask Him to break it off you, and be obedient to make the changes He has shown you. Ask the Holy Spirit to take any lies and shame from the enemy and exchange them for His truth.

Day 2:
SHAME OFTEN LEADS TO ANGER

"If you see the fruit, you have the root"

Cinda states in her book:

> "I knew I had issues but had no idea how to resolve them. At the same time, I was doing my best to stay in denial. How could a childhood incident so strongly impact my life? I certainly did not want to dwell on it or talk about it. I wanted to leave it where it was - in the past."[7]

Looking back, Cinda could see how the enemy had wrapped her in shame. The work of "shame" brings shame itself, regret, guilt, and hopelessness. It leaves you in a place where you believe you will never get free, but that is a lie of the enemy. In dealing with these situations, we tell ourselves, "It is in my past; it doesn't matter anymore – the past is the past" or maybe we just deny that it ever happened. But one thing for sure is that your life has been affected by it whether you can admit it or not. Unresolved issues often find a way of coming to the surface. Although the world says, "forget it, move on", it is not something one can easily do on their own. Too many Christians are walking around bound by shame, guilt, and regret because of something they did years ago. When something or someone triggers those feelings you have tried so hard to bury, anger can often bubble up to the surface. God wants to deal with the root of your pain. God has made a way for you to be free once and for all.

Write out Ephesians 4:26:

Scripture does not tell us to ignore our emotions. It tells us to deal with them. We need to learn how to handle our anger properly. Anger can hurt and destroy relationships. It can destroy us and make us bitter if we push it down and repress it deep within. The Apostle Paul warns us in Ephesians 4:26 to deal with our anger immediately, "before the sun goes down." When we hold onto anger, we give Satan the opportunity to destroy us and our relationships. Beth Moore put it this way in her Esther Study:

"Anger that doesn't quickly subside always ends up burning innocent people" [8]

I have been there. I remember going to the front of the church and praying and repenting over and over again, hoping that God would do something to lift off shame and guilt from me, desperately wanting to feel some release, some sense of freedom. Sometimes I did feel that freedom, but a short time later I found myself right back where I was. This repeating cycle can lead to such frustration that you become angry and take it out on those around you, who may or may not even know why you are so miserable. I remember once hearing someone say, "The most miserable person is the one who is sitting on a fence with one foot in heaven and the other in the world." It is true; you need to get off the fence. Unresolved issues need to be confronted and dealt with. It is not okay to take it out on others, and God would say it is not okay for you to take it out on yourself. Stuffing it back deep down inside, ignoring or disregarding it is not the answer. Something will eventually trigger it again, and the cycle starts over. But there is good news: Jesus can remove the root of your pain and give you freedom.

In what ways do I try to deal with the negative things that have come into my life?

God's heart is to free you of shame, guilt, regret, condemnation, and anger. God wants to lift it off you. You were not created to be cloaked or hidden in a shroud of shame. God does not put shame on you.

Read the Scriptures below and respond with what we need to do, or recognize, to rid ourselves of shame.

Psalm 22:5

Isaiah 50:7

Romans 5:5

2 Timothy 1:12

1 Peter 2:6

Hebrews 12:2 – What was the "joy set before" Jesus?

God does not look down on you with eyes of condemnation, but eyes of love. He sees you as His beloved child. Washed. Cleansed. Clothed in a robe of righteousness.

Respond to the following Scriptures by writing down how God sees you?

Psalm 34:5

2 Corinthians 5:17

2 Timothy 2:21

Isaiah 61:10

Because of what Christ has done for us and our response to His faithfulness to us, we can walk confidently knowing that God takes away the shame we or others placed on us.

Day 3:
FREEDOM IS A CHOICE

What areas in your life do you need to be made whole?

What areas could use the Lord's healing touch?

Are there any areas of my life I consider shameful?

It is God's heart for you to walk in freedom; that is why Jesus came, for your freedom! Satan wants you to believe that things will never change, that you will always be bound by strongholds, that freedom is not for you because _____ (fill in the blank). God does not hold back His love and freedom. The only one that does that is the enemy of your soul who is constantly speaking lies to you so that you will begin to identify with the lies and see them as truth. God is truth. Let Him speak His truth to you. You are chosen, and you are predestined to be His. He loves you with an everlasting love. His love never fails. His faithfulness endures forever. The one true God, Yahweh, is the key to your freedom. Allow Him to speak His truth into your life, and you will begin to walk in freedom. Stop believing the lies, start trusting Him. Freedom is a choice. When you choose to walk in God's freedom the enemy must flee.

Five Steps to Walking in Freedom

 ### Step #1: Personal Relationship With Jesus

Whether you just prayed the sinner's prayer in the introduction, or you have been walking with Jesus for years, Jesus has removed your sin and set you free.

> *"But now that you have been set free from sin and have become slaves of God, the benefit you reap leads to holiness and the result is eternal life." Romans 6:22 (NIV)*

How does God see you according to the Scriptures below?

Colossians 1:22

Isaiah 1:18

 ### Step #2: Approaching God – God Wants You to Come to Him

One of the most amazing things about being a child of God is that the Creator of the world allows us to approach Him at any time. He not only allows it, but He desires us to come to Him.

What do the following Scriptures say about approaching God?

Ephesians 3:12

Hebrews 4:16

Hebrews 10:19

You are worthy to approach the throne of God. Jesus' righteousness in you has opened the door to the throne room. I remember times in my life that I was literally afraid to approach God because I knew that my life was so messed up, and I was afraid of how badly I had disappointed him. I thought maybe He was fed up and done with me, tired of me continually choosing to sin over Him. It was easier to ignore God (pretending He did not see) than to humble myself and let the floodgates of emotions, disappointments, and frustrations flow out. Funny though, even when I did not approach Him, I felt His presence beside me in the midst of my sin, calling me back to Him. God never leaves us. He is always beside us whether we are over our head in sin or walking faithfully beside Him. He sees it all. He knows it all. A huge step to freedom is approaching God and owning up to the mess we have made and believing that God can take that mess and turn it into something beautiful, something from which we can grow.

> *"to bestow on them a crown of beauty instead of ashes, the oil of joy instead of mourning, a garment of praise for a spirit of despair." Isaiah 61:3 (NIV)*

Jesus made the way for us to talk to God. We have been given permission, through Jesus, to enter the throne room at any time and share our heart with the Father. He wants to hear from you. He wants you to open your heart to Him so He can pour right back into you all the blessings He has waiting for you. He is the giver of good gifts. Talk to him.

Step #3: Surrender Yourself to God

Please read the story of the Rich Young Ruler found in Matthew 19:16-26.

What did Jesus tell the man he needed to do to get eternal life? What was his response?

Jesus went a little deeper and told him he needed to do what? What was his response?

Jesus requires absolute surrender from His followers. To be a disciple means forsaking everything to follow Jesus unconditionally, putting our lives completely in His hands. When we say that we want to be His disciple yet attach a list of conditions of what we want, Jesus refuses to accept our terms. Jesus' terms always involve surrender. Have you turned to God in absolute surrender? What are you still holding onto? What might God be able to do through your life if you let go and followed Him no matter what the cost? What is He calling you to lay down so you can move toward what He has planned for you?

Jesus looked at the man's soul and diagnosed the condition of his heart which focused on his love for money and things over following Him. He was sitting on the fence. On the outside he was doing all the right things, but on the inside his heart was divided. His money and possessions were competing with God for his heart. He had surrendered his outward behavior to God (following the commandments), but his commitment to Him was not absolute. He had not made total surrender of himself to the Lord. I do not think Jesus was saying that we all must sell everything and give to the poor. No, he was looking into the heart of this man and saw that he had not surrendered his life completely to God. He had allowed idols (power, status, money, possessions) to become a part of his identity. This story has a sad ending:

> *"When the young man heard this, he went away sad, because he had great wealth."*
> *Matthew 19:22 (NIV)*

When faced with a choice, the man could not surrender everything. He turned his back on Jesus and walked away. Jesus' disciples looked at him and asked, "who then can be saved?" (verse 25) Jesus responded:

> *"Jesus looked at them and said, "With man this is impossible, but with God all things are possible." Matthew 19:25-26 (NIV)*

We cannot surrender on our own. We cannot get freedom on our own. We cannot be righteous on our own, but with God everything is possible. When God sees us seeking freedom in Him, His response is a "yes" and "amen". God wants to do what we deem impossible; surrender to the One who throws open the prisoner's doors and gives freedom! Do not walk away. Do not turn your back. Choose freedom.

Take some time to pray – Ask God what areas in your life have you not surrendered? Write down any thoughts or revelations the Holy Spirit speaks to you.

Surrender those things to God that God spoke to you when you prayed. If you are having difficulty doing this, ask God to help you to let go of those things that still control your life.

Cinda shares how God began to lead her to freedom:

> "I desperately wanted that freedom for myself! I sat crying next to the radio, not knowing how to proceed. Gently, I felt the Lord's presence come upon me. He was assuring me that if I dared to allow Him to take me back there, He would remain right by my side. Still, I was afraid. As I continued to sit in His presence, I slowly began to feel that I could trust Him with my pain."[9]

The enemy of our soul likes to rob us of our freedom in two ways: First, putting guilt and shame on us for situations that we had no control over, and secondly, by enslaving us in our own sin so we feel hopeless to ever be free of it.

If you are dealing with guilt and shame from a situation that you had (or have) no control over, ask God to show you the truth of the situation with which you are battling. Tell Him all the feelings and emotions you have when you think about that situation. Let it all out. Be as honest as you can so the Father can take those feelings and exchange it for truth. Once you have expressed all your thoughts, feelings, and emotions regarding the situation, ask the Father to show you the truth. Sit quietly and wait for Him to speak to you. Often the first thing you hear in your thoughts is the Father speaking. Sometimes it is one word that pops into your mind or sometimes it is a sentence or even a picture. When you believe that you have heard from God, thank Him for that word or picture He gave you, and embrace it as God's word for you. God wants you to be free, no more guilt, no more shame. Walk in your freedom.

If you are struggling with a habitual sin or stronghold (recurring destructive habits that are deeply rooted in you) that you feel hopeless to ever break, ask God directly to show you His truth.

What is it that I am gaining from this situation that keeps me coming back rather than surrendering it permanently at God's feet?

Ask God to reveal the root of your sin or stronghold? (A stronghold is a habitual sin that gets repeated over and over.)

Ask God to remove and break off any root that He reveals to you. Thank Him for His faithfulness to you.

Day 4:
WALKING IN FREEDOM

 **Step #4: To Walking in Freedom – Study His Word and Obey His Teaching**

The way to walk in freedom is to know Jesus. There is no other way.

> *"I am the way, and the truth, and the life. No one comes to the Father except through me."*
> *John 14:6 (NIV)*

Just as there is no other way to receive eternal life with the Father except through Jesus, there is no way to freedom except through Jesus. He is the way. Jesus will direct your path to freedom. He is the truth. Therefore, He will speak truth to you about yourself, your sin, and how to be free. He is the one who gives life which flows out of the knowledge of who He is and what He has done for you. Without studying the Word of God, meditating on its truth, and believing what God says about you, there will be no freedom. The Word brings life, springs of living water that refresh us. If you are not walking in freedom, it is because you have chosen to believe the lies that Satan speaks into you. Freedom comes from knowing the truth. The truth is found in God's Word.

Read the following Scriptures and respond accordingly:

Hebrews 4:12:

> *"For the word of God is alive and active. Sharper than any double-edged sword, it penetrates even to dividing soul and spirit, joints and marrow; it judges the thoughts and attitudes of the heart." (NIV)*

What does the Word of God show us when we read it?

James 1:25:

> *"But whoever looks intently into the perfect law that gives freedom and continues in it – not forgetting what they have heard but doing it – they will be blessed in what they do." (NIV)*

What gives freedom?

Why do you think "the law" gives freedom?

Colossians 3:16:

> *"Let the message of Christ dwell among you richly as you teach and admonish one another with all wisdom through psalms, hymns, and songs from the Spirit, singing to God with gratitude in your hearts." (NIV)*

What does the Word of God do?

Developing a habit of listening to God's Word keeps you from acting on impulses. When our thoughts are irrational, we need to delve into God's word for direction. His Word will bring us back onto the right path and walk us back into freedom.

> *"Your word is a lamp to my feet and a light to my path." Psalm 119:105 (NIV)*

> *"Jesus said, "If you hold to my teachings, you are really my disciples. Then you will know the truth, and the truth will set you free." John 8:31-32 (NIV)*

Day 5:
PROTECT YOUR FREEDOM

👣 Step #5: Be Vigilant to Protect Your Freedom – Do Not Let Free Will Steal Your Freedom

> *"It is for freedom that Christ has set us free. Stand firm, then, and do not let yourselves be burdened again by the yoke of slavery." Galatians 5:1 (NIV)*

Whose choice is it to be bound in slavery (in sin)?

Please read the Scriptures below:

"Live as free people, but do not use your freedom as a cover-up for evil; live as God's slaves."
1 Peter 2:16 (NIV)

"You, my brothers and sisters, were called to be free. But do not use your freedom to indulge the flesh; rather, serve one another humbly in love." Galatians 5:13 (NIV)

According to these two scriptures, what should we use our freedom for?

For what should we not use our freedom?

God has given us freedom to choose our actions and the path we want to walk in. It is our responsibility to choose wisely.

"I have the right to do anything, "you say — but not everything is beneficial. "I have the right to do anything" — but not everything is constructive. No one should seek their own good, but the good of others." 1 Corinthians 10:23-24 (NIV)

Freedom is yours, and you will have to make some changes in your life to live it out, but the new life it brings will never leave you wanting to return to the chains of the past.

Prayer for Freedom – Our Choice to Be Whole
By Cinda Gregory

"Heavenly Father, you knew me even before I was born. You know everything about me. You know the good; you know the bad. Still, you love me beyond imagination, beyond what I can grasp. Father, you even know the events of my life that I consider the most shameful. The things I have tried my best to hide from others, and yes, even tried to hide from myself ... still, You love me.

Father, I no longer want to live as a broken individual. I see "fruit" in my life that I do not like. I may not even be fully aware of what the "root" is, but I know that You do. Today, Father, I CHOOSE to trust you. I CHOOSE to allow You to come to those places that I have so closely protected and guarded, Father, I CHOOSE to partner with You to become WHOLE.

18

Would You start, right now, to gently begin to expose those areas of brokenness to me? I invite You into those places of woundedness to do what You love to do best: bring HEALING! Father, I give You permission to take me back to those places of wounding. I give You permission to remove all the hurt, all the lies that I believed in my heart, all trauma, all brokenness. As You show me this, Father, I CHOOSE to release this heavy yoke I have been carrying. I realize it was never meant for me; Jesus Christ took this yoke upon himself at Calvary. So, Jesus, I give these burdens to you. I renounce the lies that the enemy of my soul planted in my heart. Father, in place of those lies I now ask for a heavenly exchange. What truth would You like to share with me? What would You like to speak to my heart?

I release all shame, guilt, and any other feelings of defilement that the enemy cloaked me with. Father, I know You are the God of exchange. What would You like to give me in exchange for these feelings? I CHOOSE to receive them! I CHOOSE to believe Your truth. I CHOOSE to receive Your forgiveness and love as I sit here, Father, and I ask that You pour your love upon me. Wrap me in Your arms.

I sever all association and power that those "roots" and "fruits" wielded in my life. I receive the transforming power of Your love, and anxiously await the new harvest that will be rooted in Your love and wholeness. I CHOOSE, Father, to let wholeness be my lifestyle. No longer will I hide from You and Your love. You are a good, good Father, and I can trust You. Amen." [10]

Week 2:

Love Is More Than an Emotion – Choosing to Act in Love

Key #2 – Love Is a Choice

Day 1:
WHAT LOVE LOOKS LIKE

It is all about love. If the Bible could be summarized in one word, that word would be love. Love is the purpose of every chapter, every line, every story. God is love and we are to love. In the famous love chapter of the Bible, 1 Corinthians 13:3 states that without love we have nothing. We were created for love and created out of love by the Father. We have an innate craving to be loved and often will go to great lengths to attain it. Yet here is the problem: Love is not something we "get." It is something we are. Love comes from within us. It comes from the heart. It comes from your soul. It is something that must be watered and nurtured to blossom. Learning to love is so important that God wrote an entire book about it and even sacrificed His own Son so we could really know what love looks like. Love is not a feeling. It is an action.

Read 1 Corinthians 13 and write down the words that describe what love is.

Love Is Sacrifice – Love Is Servanthood

"Here is my servant whom I have chosen, the one I love, in whom I delight; I will put my Spirit on him, and he will proclaim justice to the nations." Matthew 12:18 (NIV)

Love is Servanthood – God talks a lot about servanthood in the Scriptures. His Son Jesus gave His disciples a lesson on what loving others looks like when they were together in the Upper Room. He took a towel and wrapped it around Himself and began to wash the feet of His disciples.

"…so, he got up from the meal, took off his outer clothing, and wrapped a towel around his waist. After that, he poured water into a basin and began to wash his disciples' feet, drying them with the towel that was wrapped around him." John 13:4-5. (NIV)

Feet …. dirty, smelly, cracked, calloused, hard … He chose the feet. Why feet? Perhaps they resembled their hearts. As badly as their feet needed washing, maybe their hearts needed it even more. Peter recognized this need when he said, "not just my feet but my hands and my head as well!" (John 13:9, NIV) But it was not the act of washing that was important. Peter did not understand the lesson, which was the act of serving one another. Jesus showed that ultimate love is servanthood. We allow ourselves to serve others because of our desire to express love. We choose to serve others, to carry their burdens, to somehow lighten their load. Servanthood acts can be fun and exciting! They can also be downright difficult to do. One's view of it being "fun" or "work" is found in the heart.

The heart of a servant cares more about others than self. The servant projects his or her focus, thoughts, and actions outward instead of inward. Love is unselfish. In servanthood one chooses to lay down their desires and elevates the needs of others. This seems nearly impossible in our society that thrives on self-gratification. We are taught from a young age that we are the most important person to take care of. Our world quickly begins to revolve around us, which eventually spins into chaos. God, however, has placed within us His supernatural strength, the Holy Spirit, who allows us to do the very things that are so difficult to do without Him, like putting others before ourselves.

How do the following Scriptures describe a servant?

Matthew 18:33

Matthew 20:26

Matthew 23:11

Matthew 25:21

Matthew 9:35

Mark 9:35

People quickly sense when love is lacking. When you operate out of true love for others, they feel it. They know it. Heidi Baker made the statement -- "Love looks like something."[11] Love is more than a romantic or warm feeling inside; it is an action. Loving others requires us to be willing to step out of our world into someone else's world. It is an act of the heart in surrendering to meet someone else's needs before our own. If your love is not sincere, and its goal is what you hope to get in return, it is not real love.

It is impossible to love sincerely without God because our nature is to love self. When God begins to change your heart from within, it will begin to change outside as well. Love comes from God, poured into us. Once we have experienced His unconditional love for us, we begin to have unconditional love for others. Our love is not determined by what others do, but by what God has done for us. Love breeds love. Even when people do not love you back, it does not destroy you, because any sense of rejection will be absorbed with God's great love for you. When God's love is truly in us, our love will be sincere.

When looking up Scriptures on "love" for this chapter, I was overwhelmed by how many Scriptures contained the word "love". The theme of God's love from Genesis to Revelation is the common thread that holds the Bible together. The Old Testament and New Testament are sown together by the thread of God's love for his children. Without this thread, everything would fall apart; there would be no purpose or meaning that would connect the different books together. Love is the connector: love of God for us, our love towards God and finally the love for others that flows out of the love between the first two.

The Greatest Commandment

Jesus was asked many times what was the greatest of the commandments that God had given. Jesus replied, quoting the following Scripture:

> *"Hear, O Israel: The Lord our God, the Lord is one. Love the Lord your God with all your heart and with all your soul and with all your strength. These commandments that I give you today are to be on your hearts." Deuteronomy 6:4-6 (NIV)*

With what three things are we to love God?

Read Deuteronomy 10:12

"And now, O Israel, what does the Lord your God ask of you but to fear the Lord your God, to walk in all his ways, to love him, to serve the Lord your God with all your heart and with all your soul." (NIV)

What four actions does God tell us to do?

How are we to do these things?

As soon as Christ answered the first question, He immediately followed His first response by stating the second greatest commandment:

"Teacher, which is the greatest commandment in the Law?" Jesus replied: "Love the Lord your God with all your heart and with all your soul and with all your mind. This is the first and greatest commandment." And the second is like it: "Love your neighbor as yourself. All the Law and the Prophets hang on these two commandments." Matthew 22:36-40 (NIV)

Explain in your own words what it means that "on these two commandments depend all the Law and Prophets" at the end of verse 40.

We are called to love by the God who created us. He designed us to be "loving," to bear the character trait of who He is, love. Love breeds love. "Because God loved us first," we can love others.

Day 2:
REFLECTING THE FATHER'S LOVE REQUIRES ACTION

How are we supposed to love?

"Dear children, let us not love with words or speech but with actions and in truth." 1 John 3:18 (NIV)

Jesus taught us how to love by His actions. In the book of Matthew, we were introduced to John the Baptist. John was the prophet sent to prepare the way for Jesus.

"A voice of the one calling in the wilderness, "Prepare the way for the Lord, make straight paths for him."" *Matthew 3:3 (NIV)*

And then it happened. John came face to face with the One he was announcing.

"Then Jesus came from Galilee to the Jordan to be baptized by John. But John tried to deter him, saying, "I need to be baptized by you, and do you come to me?" Matthew 3:13-14 (NIV)

"As soon as Jesus was baptized, he went up out of the water. At that moment heaven was opened, and he saw the Spirit of God descending like a dove and alighting on him.[17] And a voice from heaven said, "This is my Son, whom I love; with him I am well pleased." Matthew 3:16-17 (NIV)

When John the Baptist was in prison, he heard what Jesus was DOING, so he sent his disciples to ask Him, "Are you the one who was to come, or should we expect someone else?" (Matthew 11:3, NIV) Even John had wanted to make sure. He may have had doubts, or maybe he just wanted to confirm what he believed. Whatever the reason that caused John to doubt or question, would soon vanish.

Please read Matthew 11:2-5 and write down the things Jesus told John's disciples.

Jesus wanted John to have no doubts. He answered him by telling him what He was doing and how people were responding. With so much evidence, Jesus' identity would be obvious to John, and he could rest in the knowledge that he had done his job and that the Messiah was here. Love requires more than words. It requires action. It is only in our actions that love can be seen by others. For us to be able to love the way God desires us to love, we may need to lay some things down at the throne of the Father.

Ask yourself – "Am I willing to change and allow myself to love others the way God designed me to love?" What holds me back?

As Cinda stated in her book, "Love is not simply an emotion; it is something I can choose and act on"[12] Am I willing to step out of my comfort zone and choose to love by touching others through my actions?

To Love Completely Action Is Necessary

Throughout the remainder of the week, we will look at seven things we need to do to walk in love.

♥ 1. To Love – You Need to Lay Down Sin

You cannot love if you are self-absorbed. We must stop the attitude that sin only affects me - someone else is always affected by your sin. Sin is like the pebble thrown into the still lake that is so smooth it looks like a mirror. When the pebble hits the water, the ripples start out small, but then continue to extend farther and farther out. Sin has a "ripple effect."

Pray – Ask God where your sin has hurt other people and seek His forgiveness.

What does He want you to do in response to His revelation?

He may lead you to seek the forgiveness from the person you hurt, or He may just work things out in you. Your sin may appear like a small pebble to you, but it could become a rock to someone else. Listen to your Father, He will direct you. God wants you to be free to love others. This is the first essential step to loving.

♥ 2. To Love You Must Believe Sincerity Matters

God wants our love towards Him to be sincere. He also wants that same sincere love to be expressed to others through us. Sincerity is being truthful without deceit or hypocrisy.

Read Romans 12:9 – What is the first statement made?

Describe what the word "sincere" means to you.

Read the rest of the Romans 12:9-21. List some of the examples of sincere love.

God sees your heart, and He wants you to know that sincerity matters. Cinda made this statement about what she thought about sin when she was first saved: "I had a very shallow view of Christ's

sacrifice and what being a disciple entailed. My theology was simple: I said a prayer, was forgiven and earned my ticket to heaven. I figured that sinning was no big deal, as all I had to do was recite another quick prayer, ask to be forgiven, and everything would once again be great. However, now that I was personally experiencing the ramifications of my deceptive actions and poor decisions, I was starting to rethink my belief system."[13]

The problem with this is that it is "premeditated sin". When we choose to revisit the same sin over and over, we are not truly seeking repentance. We fully anticipate sinning again – repentance is turning away and never doing it again. God's grace and forgiveness is extended to us every moment of everyday, all we must do is accept it with a pure heart. The heart attitude means something to God. Being sincere with God and being sincere with others is critical to loving. God knows if we are sincere or not and so will others. Seek to be sincere.

When we seek forgiveness without true repentance, we mock what Christ has done on the cross. God will not be mocked. Neither will He be deceived. He sees right through us.

It is only when we seek Him with all our heart that we will find Him.

Read Jeremiah 29:13-14a and fill in the blanks:

"And you will seek Me and find Me when you _____ Me with _____ your heart. I will be _____ by you; says the Lord and I will _____ you _____ from captivity." (NIV)

What areas of my life have I allowed sin to continue while I hold onto an attitude that God will forgive me? He understands my heart and my struggle.

What is holding you back from receiving God's complete love for you?

Obedience is often spoken in conjunction with sincerity of heart. "If you love Me, keep my commands." (John 14:15, NIV) Cinda speaks about the time she read this Scripture and how truth pierced her heart. "Suddenly, it seemed love had less to do with how a person felt, and more to do with what the person did. I could not believe it. It was the opposite of what I had always believed. Here, in this Scripture, God was saying if you loved Him, you did something – you kept His commandments. Love was an action, not a feeling like I had always believed. The evidence of the love was action, not the warm and fuzzy chick-flick feeling I had always imagined. God again spoke to my heart saying that if I took action, the feelings would eventually follow, but they were not to be my barometer."[14]

What do the following Scriptures say about sincere love?

Colossians 3:22–23

1 Peter 1:22

Hebrews 10:22

Sincere love involves selfless giving; a self-centered person cannot genuinely love. God's love and forgiveness allows us to take our eyes off ourselves to meet other's needs. Through Christ's sacrifice we can see His sacrificial love for us. Now we can take His example of sincere love and give ourselves sacrificially for others.

Day 3:
TO LOVE LET GOD BE JUDGE –
CHOOSING NOT TO BE OFFENDED

♥ 3. To Love Is to Let God Be the Judge

"Revenge leads to regret – regret does not take away the pain of the devastation."[15]

Seeking revenge is not yours to do. God is the one who sits on the throne, and it is His job to make sure that justice is done. We can rest assured that God will make things right before our accusers or before those who tormented us on earth. Letting it go into the Father's care will keep us from becoming bitter, angry, and cynical. It will allow us the freedom to "love" regardless of what has happened in the past.

Read the following Scriptures and answer the questions.

"*There is a judge for the one who rejects me and does not accept my words; that very word which I spoke will condemn him at the last day.*" *John 12:48 (NIV)*

There is a _____ .

"Then I saw a great white throne and him who was seated on it. Earth and sky fled from his presence, and there was no place for them. And I saw the dead, great and small, standing before the throne, and books were opened. Another book was opened, which is the book of life. The dead were judged according to what they had done as recorded in the books. The sea gave up the dead that were in it, and death and Hades gave up the dead that were in them, and each person was judged according to what he had done." Revelation 20:11-13 (NIV)

Who did John see and where was He?

What does verse 12b say:

What two books were opened?

Read Romans 2:1-16: What is God's judgement based on?

What does God's kindness lead us to?

What does stubbornness and an unrepentant heart lead to?

Write down verse 8:

God is the only one who knows the truth and hearts of man. We are to believe God's Word when He tells us that He takes care of the judging and justice that needs to be done. Leave it in His hands and let it go.

♥ 4. To Love Is Choosing to Not Be Offended

We are called to love like Jesus, regardless of if they love you back. Choose to act in love, regardless of whether feelings are there or not. If you do, the feelings will eventually follow. Choose not to be offended by others.

What are the main points of each Scripture below?

Proverbs 19:11

Ezekiel 33:10

Proverbs 17:9

We are to be careful about not taking offense from others, but also, we need to watch that we are not offensive to others by our attitude or actions.

Psalm 139:24

Ezekiel 18:30-32

Day 4:
LOVE COMPELS YOU TO GIVE YOUR ALL

❤ 5. To Love We Need to Spend Time in God's Presence

When we spend time in God's presence, we cannot help but be changed. The way we interact with others will be impacted whether we are aware of it or not.

❤ 6. Love Compels You to Give Your All

Please read Luke 7:36-50 – The story of the woman who washed Jesus' feet with her tears and wiped them with her hair.

> *"…a woman of the streets – a prostitute – heard he was there and brought an exquisite flask filled with expensive perfume. Going in, she knelt behind him at his feet, and she wiped them off with her hair and kissed them and poured the perfume on them." Luke 7:36-38 (The Living Bible)*

This was not the first encounter this woman had had with Jesus. In verse 37 notice the words "had lived" and in verse 47 "her many sins have been forgiven." This woman had already received forgiveness from Jesus. Her purpose for coming was to worship him. She knew the great love of Jesus. He had rescued her from her sinful life and her overflowing love was a natural response for the forgiveness she had received. She knew the depth of her sin which made His love even more precious. She could have been stuck in the pit of adultery forever, yet God's love would not allow her to remain there. Neither will His love allow you to remain in your sin. When you cry out for forgiveness, it reaches the Father's ears, and His right arm reaches out to you and pulls you up out of the muck and mire, declaring you are forgiven. The greater the need for forgiveness, the stronger the love for the Father. Jesus confronted His disciples as they watched the scene unfold with distain on their faces:

What was Jesus' response in Luke 7:47?

When you know that you are utterly helpless to help yourself, and God chooses to help you, aren't you overwhelmed with gratitude? Words cannot express the thankfulness in your heart. This was Mary. She had to pour out her love because Jesus had poured so much into her that her heart and her love and gratitude were overflowing. She was compelled to show her love, her thankfulness. Her heart would never forget what Jesus had done for her.

The Story of the Woman Who Anoints Jesus With Perfume

This is another story of a woman compelled by love. Although, both women were named Mary, this Mary is the sister of Martha and Lazarus. These three were like family to Jesus and Jesus often stayed with them at Martha's home. Mary's overwhelming love for Jesus was displayed by her anointing Jesus' body to prepare Him for His burial.

Read Mark 14:3-9: What did Mary do?

How did the others in the room react?

How did Jesus respond to her act of love in verse 6?

Reread verse 8 and write it below:

Mary gave her best, "An alabaster jar of very expensive perfume, made of pure nard." (Mark 14:3 NIV) It was not just what was in the jar, but the jar itself had value. The jar was made of a rich marble-type stone (alabaster or translucent gypsum) that was soft enough to carve. This alabaster stone was considered a precious stone in Israel and was used to decorate King Solomon's temple. The jar was filled with the expensive perfume and then the neck of the jar would be sealed with a wax to ensure that the perfume would remain pure and unspoiled until needed. Once the jar was broken, the entire contents must be poured out and used, otherwise it would spoil. There was no putting it back, once the neck of the jar was broken. The perfume Mary had in her jar was spikenard – pure nard. Spikenard was considered the very best in ancient cultures. So, when Mary broke the alabaster jar and poured out the oil over Jesus she was honoring Jesus with the most valuable thing she had to offer, she gave her best to him out of her great love and devotion to him. Jesus responded to the love that was being displayed in her actions. He called it beautiful. When God sees us loving others through our actions, He sees it as beautiful. Jesus praised Mary for her unselfish act of worship. Mary worshiped Jesus with utmost love, respect, honor and devotion and was willing to sacrifice to Him what was most precious. Her heart would not allow her to do anything less – she, too, was compelled by love.

What was the most extravagant gift you every gave somebody?

What motivated you to give that person such a gift?

Read the Story of the Poor Widow who Gives all she has in Mark 12:41-44.

Write down verse 44 below.

In Jesus' eyes this widow gave more than all the others put together, though her gift was the smallest. Not only was this woman a poor widow, but she also had few resources for making money. Her small gift was a sacrifice, but she gave it willingly. The true value of the gift given is determined by the spirit in which it is given, not by the monetary amount. We do not know anything else about this widow, except that her sacrificial action showed her love for God – she was compelled to give out of her great love. A gift of any size is pleasing to God when given out of joy, gratitude, and a heart full of generosity.

Jesus was the greatest example of love in action. He constantly displayed His love for people: He healed the sick, raised the dead, fed the hungry, comforted those who mourned, gave people more than they could ask for (fishermen and their great catch), bound up the broken hearted, accepted the rejected, cast out demons and ultimately gave His life for us by dying on the cross. And even on the cross, He acted in love when the criminal rebuked the other criminal and said:

> *"Don't you fear God since you are under the same sentence? We are punished justly, for we are getting what our deeds deserved. But this man has done nothing wrong." Then he said, "Jesus, remember me when you come into your kingdom." And Jesus responded, "I tell you the truth, today you will be with me in paradise." Luke 23:40-43 (NIV)*

He did not stop loving. Jesus was compelled by love to die – for the criminal and for you. Love is sacrificial; it requires us to give up "self" and put others first.

We are called to love others like Jesus, regardless of whether they love you back. Choose to act in love, regardless of if the feelings are there or not. Choose not to be offended by others. Is there someone in your life that needs to be shown love through action? What holds you back from stepping out and being obedient to the Father? God will give you the strength to choose to love if you ask Him. He desires for you to be loving. He can move the mountains. He can make the stones cry out. He can transform your heart and fill it to overflowing with love if you allow Him to work in you.

What do the following Scriptures tell you about God's plans?

Ephesians 3:20-21

1 Corinthians 2:9

He has so much more that He wants to give you that you cannot even imagine. All his plans are created out of His great love for you. He wants to blow your mind with more than you could ever imagine. Will you allow His love to take over your life? Will you be an agent of His love to the world around you? This leads to our last point, which is critical for God to move.

Day 5:
BELIEVING GOD

♥ 7. To Love You Must "Believe" God

Do you believe God will do what He says He will do? Do you take Scripture seriously? You may have heard it said that you cannot pick and choose what you want to believe from the Bible. It is true, we embrace some Scriptures and dismiss others, especially those we do not understand or simply do not like. When a time comes to stand in belief, we hear ourselves crying out to the Lord, "I do believe; help me overcome my unbelief." (Mark 9:24 NIV) One of the hardest questions to ask ourselves is whether we believe the Word of God, from the first word of Genesis to the last word of Revelation? Our actions will often answer this question for us. When I pondered this question for the first time, I found myself struggling with my answer. I wanted it to be "yes" so badly. But, when I looked at the world and read the Word of God, I often did not see His promises being fulfilled in situations that surrounded me. My faith could be described as a roller coaster, up and down depending on what I believed.

> "I have spoken to you of earthly things and you do not believe, how then will you believe if I speak of heavenly things?" John 3:12 (NIV)

Do I believe God is good to those who love Him? Do I believe God is forgiving and has really wiped away my past when I can't even forgive myself? Do I believe that "God is faithful" regardless of what my eyes see? Where is the disconnect? Do I believe what the Word of God says or don't I? Do I try to explain it away somehow, "that was then, it doesn't apply to us," or, "that is something that will take place in the future, when we are home in heaven?" But then the Scripture says, "Thy kingdom come ON earth as it is in heaven." God wants to bring heaven down to earth today, not just when He returns and establishes the New Jerusalem.

God is calling us to believe His Word even if we do not see it playing out before our eyes. That is why it requires faith; we believe what God says regardless of what our eyes do or do not see.

Read John 4:46-54 – Jesus Heals a Government Official's Son

What did the government official ask Jesus to do?

What did Jesus tell the man?

What was the man's response right after Jesus said this?

The official had faith that Jesus could do what He claimed. The official believed, THEN he saw a miracle. The official obeyed Jesus out of his belief that Jesus will do what He says He will do. It is not enough to say we believe Jesus can take care of our problems. We need to believe He will. When you pray about a need or problem, live as though you believe Jesus will do what He says.

Do I believe that God will do what His Word says He will do?

As a result of his actions, the official's faith grew and what was the result? (John 4:53)

In Romans 12:3 we are told that we are all given a measure of faith. Faith (believing) is a gift that grows as you use it. As we walk in faith, we develop a mindset that expects God to act (not according to what we demand, but in accordance with His promises, His Word, and His character) As we develop confidence in God's faithfulness, we begin to walk in the expectation that God is in control, and we no longer have to walk in worry, fear and anxiety. The parable of the mustard seed reminds us that faith as small as a mustard seed may have small beginnings but will bring great rewards. (Matthew 13:31-32, NIV) The more you exercise your faith in action, the more you will grow.

When was the last time you exercised your faith?

What was the result of your action?

The three Scriptures below have helped me work through this question of believing God. God knows what a struggle "believing" can be for us.

> *"For my thoughts are not your thoughts, neither are your ways my ways declares the Lord. As the heavens are higher than the earth, so are my ways higher than your ways and my thoughts than your thoughts." Isaiah 55:8-9 (NIV)*

> *"Trust in the Lord with all your heart and lean not on your own understanding." Proverbs 3:5 (NIV)*

34

"The work of God is this; to believe in the one he has sent." John 6:29 (NIV)

We are not going to understand it all, we were never meant to. We are called to believe what God says in His Word and to stand on His promises and call them down from heaven to earth. Did you notice in the Scripture above that the work of God is "to believe"? Faith and believing takes work. The more we study God's Word, the more we begin believing that if God said it, He meant it, and He will bring whatever He has promised or said to pass.

Some of you are struggling with these thoughts; you just are not sure what you believe. Go to the Father and ask Him to speak to you. Open the Word and look up Scriptures that speak about the areas you are struggling in and ask God to reveal His truth to you. Write down any promises that God speaks in those Scriptures (they are for you). Write down what God says about it. Write down any Scripture that jumps off the page at you and meditate on it and then apply that Scripture to your life. Start believing that God wants to move in your life and start believing that He has an amazing plan for you. Will you choose to join Him in His work? Will you allow Him to finish the work that He began in you? He has great plans for you, do you believe it? It is time we start believing what God has spoken. "He is the same yesterday, today and tomorrow."

Along with the thread of love, there are two other threads woven throughout the Scriptures: the threads of hope and faith. When faith, hope and love are woven together as a strand of three, our love will stand firm and not be shaken. We will be a ready vessel to be used by the Lord. It is alright to cry out like the father of the son who was possessed by a spirit: "I do believe; help me overcome my unbelief." (Mark 9:23-24 (NIV) God already knows our struggles, that is why He spends so much time in Scripture talking about faith and believing. God wants to make us strong. God will help us to stand firm.

Loving God's Community

"A new command I give to you; love one another. As I have loved you, so you must love
one another. By this all men will know that you are my disciples if you love one another."
John 13:34-35 (NIV)

It is a command from Jesus – to love like Jesus. A sacrificial love. A love that chooses to…

- Love when it is not convenient.
- Love by giving when it hurts.
- Love by devoting your energy to serve others.
- Love by absorbing the hurts you experience from others without complaining or fighting back.

- Love others by meeting any need that you can.
- Love others by having compassion, mercy, and sincere concern for them.
- Love others by praying for them unceasingly.

Peter wrote to his Christian brothers and sisters scattered amongst the nations to walk in love.

What do the following Scriptures tell us about loving people?

1 Peter 3:8-9

1 Peter 4:8

We were never meant to navigate trials alone – we need each other, the community of God. When the community of God works together and perseveres, great advancement for the Kingdom of God comes down to the earth, "Thy will be done ON EARTH as it is in heaven." We are called to bring the kingdom of heaven to earth, the kingdom of love.

God is calling you to join Him along with your brothers and sisters to accomplish His will on this earth. He will equip you with all you need. He will guide and direct you. He will train you. If you partner with Him, you will experience things you never dreamed possible, for God is the God of the impossible.

What does Ephesians 3:20 say God wants to do?

Whose power accomplishes the work?

Love in action is what we are called to do and be. It is the love that changes us first, then those around us and then the world. I think of the saying "better together." That is what we are when believers work together to show the love of the Father to this hurting world. We are empowered by God's love which compels us to love like Him. He will use you. You just need to step out believing He will do what He says He will do.

God is looking for believers that believe Him and what He says. He wants to partner with us. When Jesus was raised from the dead, He came to His disciples and imparted His authority to them and

to us. He has given us permission to minister in His name, using the power that comes along with it. Embrace the authority and power that Jesus won for us.

Let me end with a quote from evangelist Todd White – "Just Be Jesus – Just Be Love."[16]

Prayer for Choosing to Love
By Cinda Gregory

"Heavenly Father, it is your desire to be the Lover of our souls and teach us what true love is. I confess that I have often chosen not to act in love. I repent of that and ask Your forgiveness. Father, I am not even sure that I truly understand love as you see it…I choose to open my heart to Your presence. Would you teach me to love like You do? With no agenda and no strings attached.

Father, it is impossible to love others if we do not first know that You love us. So, I choose to open my heart to Your love. Would you show me how much You love me? Surround me and envelop me with Your love and presence. Speak to my heart and tell me of Your love. Still my heart, Father, as I allow You to minister to me. Touch me deep in my heart, where no man can touch. Thank you, Daddy.

Father, if there are areas in my heart where I have felt rejected and unloved, would you increase Your presence right now and heal those areas of my heart? I ask You to re-nurture me in those areas of hurt and exchange them with Your love and presence? Thank you, Daddy.

Now Father, I ask that you see me as an instrument of love and healing to others. Out of the abundance of love that You have poured into my heart, I ask that it overflow to all those around me. Let my actions of love change the lives of others. I bring all my current and future relationships before Your Throne and ask You to bless and prosper them as I choose to be a living instrument of love in Your hands.

Your Word says that You do exceedingly and abundantly more than we can ever expect or imagine, so Father, I am asking that You do that for me and my relationships. Change me and use me to change the world around me! Amen." [17]

Week 3:
Removing the Mask –
Choosing Transparency and Vulnerability

Key #3 – Transparency Is a Choice

Day 1:
WHERE ARE YOU?

I never did like masks. I loved to play dress up, but masks were never in my make-believe wardrobe. I always wanted to see a face, to know who was there with me. Seeing someone's face gave me comfort, made me feel safe. I have not changed much. I still want to see the faces of those around me. It has been said, "The eyes are the windows to the soul." My mother-in-law had eyes that literally twinkled and danced. She loved life and her eyes reflected the joy within her. The eyes truly are windows to our soul. They often express our emotions buried deep within. There was a time I used to wear a sort of mask. A Christian retreat I went to introduced me to liturgical clowns. I had never seen a liturgical clown before. I only knew of circus clowns from my childhood experiences. But these clowns were different, and they were not necessarily funny; their job was not to make you laugh but to think. There was no talking, so it was only the actions that spoke the message with the use of props. The message always spoke of some aspect of God the Father or Jesus. Quite often it demonstrated God as the healer of the broken hearted, the one who set captives free, the restorer of hope. All the skits were thought-provoking, as the clowns themselves became the heart, hands, and eyes of Jesus. I think it was the eyes that got to me the most. When looking into the clown's eyes I could see the "love of the Father" looking right at me. His loving eyes were looking right into my heart and bringing healing to my soul, stripping away the masks I carried deep within. I was so touched that I became a liturgical clown.

The white face we put on was not to hide behind, but it was to take away man's face and to represent the Father's face. The "white face" symbolized becoming dead to ourselves, and the colors we applied to our face made us alive in Christ. Creating my face was up to me. What message did I

38

RECLAIMING YOUR DESTINY

want my face to portray? My face had a cross over the one eye with a red heart at the bottom of it and the other eye became a fish (fisher of men). On my cheek were colors of the rainbow in glitter. I love glitter, always have, so my clown's name became "Sparkle". My hair was bright pink – it was lots of fun, and so is God. Whenever we presented our skits, we would take on a different character, but my face never changed. Whatever role we played in the skit, there was always someone depicting God as the loving Father. God always showed up by touching the audience in ways that words never could. People often came in struggling and left with a new sense of freedom. When we put our faces on, and put on the face of the Father, people in our audience would take their "masks" off and let God do his work in their lives.

Jesus always removes the mask if we allow Him. He does not want us hiding. Hiding is never a good thing. It keeps us wrapped in a cloud of fear, guilt and shame. We hide ourselves in many ways: pretending to be something we are not, burying our emotions and feelings deep down so no one will see them, putting up walls so people can only go so far in getting to know us, putting our energy into a lot of things (work, hobbies, service) to keep us busy so we do not have to deal with "ourselves" and the wounds we are carrying. It is time to let God heal those inner wounds.

God has His eye on all His creation. Although man has tried, you cannot hide from God. Even some of the more famous characters in the Bible tried hiding from God. It did not work. God always knew where and why they were hiding. David learned quickly that he could never be separated from the presence of God. David proclaims this wonderful fact in Psalm 139:7-10:

> *"Where can I go from your Spirit? Where can I flee from your presence? If I go up to the heavens, you are there; if I make my bed in the depths, you are there. If I rise on the wings of the dawn, if I settle on the far side of the sea, even there your hand will guide me, your right hand will hold me fast." (NIV)*

Please read the Scriptures below and complete the answers.

Genesis 3:8-10 – What did the Lord ask Adam and Eve in verse 9?

Why were they hiding?

Read 1 Samuel 10:17-27 – Saul being Chosen to be King.

What did the Israelites ask God for?

What did Samuel do?

Who was chosen to be King?

Where was Saul and what was he doing?

Why do you think he was hiding?

1 Kings 19:3-4 – The Story of Elijah the Famous Prophet
Why was Elijah hiding?

Who came to Elijah and what did he do for him? (Verses 5-8)

What did Elijah do next? Where did he end up? (Verse 9)

What did the Lord say to him?

God said to Elijah, *"What are you doing here, Elijah?"* (1 Kings 19:9 NIV) Perhaps, He is asking us the same question. Why do we hide from God? God will always come to find us. He is the Good Shepherd, and He is always looking for those that are lost, or, in this case, hiding. God does not want you to hide. He desires you seek Him when you are afraid and when you do not know what to do next. If you are walking with God, you need not fear. His *"perfect love casts out all fear."* (1 John 4:18 NIV) Sometimes we become so focused on the world around us, and how it is deteriorating, that we do not realize the deterioration of our own soul. It is when we are alone, as Elijah was on

Mount Horeb, that our transparency draws the presence of God near us. God wants to lavish love on you; there is no need to hide or be fearful. His love will conquer all things. His love will fight for you. His love will cover you and surround you. His love will make you strong and courageous. No more hiding among the baggage, or in a cave, or in the crowds, or in our silence. God knows you and where you are, so do not fear. God's love gives us the ability to be transparent and vulnerable. Yes, that can be scary, but freedom comes when we are real. When we walk in transparency, we are set free from the fear of being exposed. No more masks, no more hiding, no more deception. It is time to be transparent and vulnerable, especially with God.

Definition of *transparent* (by Websters Dictionary):

Fine or sheer enough to be seen through

Readily understood, easy to notice

Free from pretense or deceit

Easily detected or seen through/obvious

Visibility or accessibility

Honest and open, not secretive

Does not lie

Allowing light to pass through so that the object behind can be distinctly seen[18]

Definition of *vulnerable* (by Websters Dictionary):

Capable of being physically or emotionally wounded

Open to attack or damage

Exposed, endangered

Open, sensitive

Liable[19]

As I read through these definitions, I felt more comfortable with being transparent than with being vulnerable. It sounds so risky because it is. Did you notice the last definition of transparency? "Allowing light to pass through so that the object behind can be distinctly seen." Being vulnerable and transparent is not something that we naturally do. It is something that God develops in us, so ultimately His glory shines through our lives so purely that others see Him.

Let us look at three people in the Bible that were challenged in choosing whether or not to be transparent and vulnerable. The struggle is real, but victory is sweet for those who overcome and choose vulnerability and transparency over deception.

Day 2:
THE GREAT PRETENDERS
The Pharisees – The Mask of Hypocrisy

Portraying a False Identity:
Pretending to Be One Thing When You Are Really Not

Jesus was constantly confronting the Pharisees on the words they spoke and how they applied Scripture in contrast to their actions. What they said and what they did were often two different things. For the Pharisees, their mask was hiding behind their position and the political power that came with being priests. They knew all the Scriptures, they knew the laws given to Moses, but they never internalized them. The Pharisees' weakness was that they were content to obey outwardly without allowing God to change their hearts or attitudes inside. They looked pious, but they were far from the Kingdom of God. God judges our hearts as well as our deeds, for it is in the heart our real allegiance lies. We should be just as concerned about the attitudes that people do not see as those actions that are seen by all. We can learn a lot about how God wants us to live by looking at the Pharisees.

Please read the Scriptures below and complete the blanks with the appropriate word. Scriptures are taken from the New International Version.

Mark 7:6:

"He replied, "Isaiah was right when he prophesied about you hypocrites; as it is written: "These people _____ me with their lips, but their _____ are far from me." (NIV)

Matthew 23:27:

"Woe to you, teachers of the law and Pharisees, you hypocrites! You are like _____ tombs, which look _____ on the _____ but on the inside are full of the _____ of the _____ and everything _____ ." (NIV)

What does God see when He Searches Our Hearts? Read the Scripture and complete the blanks.

Hebrews 4:12:

"For the word of God is alive and active. Sharper than any double-edged sword, it penetrates even to dividing soul and spirit, joints and marrow; it judges the _____ and _____ of the _____ ." (NIV)

1 Chronicles 28:9:

"And you my son Solomon, acknowledge the God of your father, and serve him with wholehearted devotion and with a willing mind, for the Lord searches every heart and understands _____ behind the thoughts. If you seek him, he will be found by you; but if you forsake him, he will reject you forever." (NIV)

Read 1 Samuel 16:6-7 – God sent Samuel to anoint David as king. What were God's specific instructions to Samuel?

What did God tell Samuel not to do?

How does God see man?

Fill in the blanks to complete the Scriptures below.

Psalm 51:17

"The sacrifices of God are a _____ spirit; a _____ and _____ heart, O God. you will not despise." (English Standard Version)

Isaiah 57:15

"For this is what the high and exalted One says- he who lives forever, whose name is holy: "I live in a high and holy place, but also with the one who is _____ and _____ in spirit, to _____ the spirit of the lowly and to _____ the heart of the contrite." (NIV)

God has never stopped looking at the heart. We do not ever deceive God with what we portray in our outward appearance. He sees right through our masks and our hypocrisy and knows what is truly inside of us. Do our words and actions line up with what we believe, or are we portraying a false identity?

So how did it turn out for the Pharisees? When Jesus confronted their hypocrisy and the false image they were portraying, they became indignant and angry. Their pride would not let Jesus' words sink deep into their hearts. Instead, their hearts were hardened to the point of plotting to kill Jesus.

The Story of Jacob and Esau
Please read Genesis 25:27-34

Both Jacob and Esau were "drama queens" or, I should say, "drama kings." Jacob jumped on the opportunity and decided to take advantage of his brother's dramatic declaration that he was famished and about to die. He suggested that Esau sell him his birthright for the bowl of stew. Esau agreed and traded his birthright away as he devoured the stew. Esau operated out of a momentary desire and Jacob embraced the role of cheating and deceiving his brother. To make matters worse, their own mother Rebekah made a deceptive plan after listening to her husband Isaac tell Esau to bring him some food and then he would pronounce his blessing over him. Rebekah plotted the plan, and Jacob put on the mask. No one embraced honesty in this story; God had already said that Jacob would receive the blessing. Rebekah and Jacob took things into their own hands and did not allow God to work His timing out.

What plan did Jacob agree to take part in according to Genesis 27:5-29?

Jacob literally put on a costume, a mask of deception, to steal His father's (Isaac's) blessing from his brother Esau. Both Esau and Jacob reaped severe consequences for their actions. They each saw an opportunity to get something they wanted, and their first impulse was to get it. The immediate pleasure one seeks often loses sight of the future. The pressure of the moment can distort your perspective and make you feel a decision is urgent. When feeling a tremendous amount of pressure in one area of our lives, we often can no longer focus on anything else, which can cause us to lose our perspective. As a result, the consequences can be devastating.

What actions did the main characters take and describe the fallout for each character?

Jacob – Read Genesis 27:18-43; 29:16-27; 31:20; 32:8-11

44

Esau – Read Genesis 25:32-34; 27:30-34; 27:41; 28:6-9

Rebekah – Genesis 27:8-10; 27:42-45

Have you ever made a spur of the moment decision under pressure that you regretted later?

What were the consequences of that decision?

Getting through that short, pressure-filled moment is often the most difficult part of overcoming a temptation. To avoid the same mistakes as Esau, make sure you compare the short-term satisfaction with the long-term consequences BEFORE you act. How we react to a moral dilemma often reveals our real motives. Are we more concerned about getting caught than being deceitful? If you are in a position that you are worried about being caught, then you are most likely in a position that is less than honest and probably is deceitful and sinful. The fear of getting caught has saved many people from doing devastating things that they later regret. Think before you act on impulse. Do not be deceived into thinking that you can get away with sin and not reap consequences from your deception.

The Great Reunion

Read Genesis Chapters 32-33 – a close-up view of Jacob and Esau's reunion.

What was Jacob's reaction when he heard his brother was coming to meet him?

His plan was not necessary because, as we see in the next chapter, somewhere through their time apart Esau had worked through his anger, forgiven his brother and had a change of heart. The bitterness Esau had over losing his father's blessing and his birthright were gone. Jacob was dreading the reunion with his brother and Esau was anticipating it.

Genesis 33:3-5 shows us how the reunion unfolded. Describe this scene in your own words.

Jacob showed humility by bowing before his brother seven times. Forgiveness always requires humility and transparency, and Jacob was quick to show it to his brother. Transparency and humility strip off the mask of deception and allow for deep healing to begin.

Joseph's Story – When Opportunity Knocks
Read Genesis 37:1-36 – The Story of Joseph

Joseph had it all. His parents were Rachel and Jacob. He had ten older brothers and one younger brother, but *"Israel (Jacob) loved Joseph more than any of his other sons, because he had been born to him in his old age."* (Genesis 37:3 NIV) Israel made Joseph a richly ornamented robe. As a result, *"When his brothers saw that their father loved him more than any of them, they hated him, and could not speak a kind word to him."* Genesis 37:4 (NIV) Joseph had a way of approaching his brothers with an attitude of being better than them (after all, his father planted that seed in him). He flaunted his beautiful robe that his father gave him. Then he felt the need to share his dreams with them which made his brothers jealous and began the devastating road ahead for Joseph. His brothers had quite enough of Joseph and plotted to kill him. Joseph's life seemed to be spiraling out of control.

Joseph's life was packed full of drama. His story begins with his brothers' plot to get rid of him and fabricating the details of his disappearance to their father. Their deception went on for years until they came face to face with their brother as second-in-command of Egypt. Throughout the years Joseph did not let his past immobilize him from accomplishing things. He worked extremely hard. He always did his best and was known as a man of integrity. God's hand was upon him, and he was shown favor by all those he worked for or who surrounded him.

Read the Scriptures and record the events that happened to Joseph.

Genesis 37:18-27

Genesis 39:1-20

Genesis 40:8-23

Genesis 41:25-39

Genesis 41:37-42

Genesis 41:53-56

In Genesis 41, the time came for which God had prepared Joseph throughout all those years. His dream was about to unfold. After Joseph interpreted the king's dream, Joseph was made second-in-command over Egypt. He had filled the storehouses with grain and was now in charge of parceling out the food to those who came for help. Little did he know his brothers were on their way. In Genesis 42, Joseph's brothers again enter the story, thirteen years after they sold Joseph into slavery. Jacob sends his sons to Egypt to buy grain, and unbeknownst to them, they will be coming face to face with their brother, Joseph. Joseph's brothers arrive and bow down to him with their faces to the ground. As soon as Joseph sees his brothers, he recognizes them, but they do not recognize him. This is Joseph's big moment. "Opportunity is knocking at his door." Will Joseph come clean and reveal who he is, or will he take this opportunity for a little "payback" for what his brothers had done to him?

Read Genesis 42:7 below:

"As soon as Joseph saw his brothers, he recognized them, but he pretended to be a stranger and spoke harshly to them." (NIV)

Did you catch that? What did Joseph do? Joseph pretended to be a stranger. He purposely chose not to reveal his true identity to his brothers. He was now wearing the mask of deception as he talked to his brothers.

Why do you think Joseph pretended?

Realizing his brothers did not recognize him, he quickly developed a plan that would allow him to get his entire family reunited with him. I am sure that Joseph was now realizing the denial and pain he had buried for years. He yearned for reconciliation, but before that would happen Joseph could not help but make his brothers squirm a little, or maybe even more than a little.

Please read Genesis 42:8 – Genesis 44 – What did Joseph do to his brothers while not revealing who he really was to them?

Do you think it was right? Yes, or no? Please explain your answer.

The brothers returned home with the grain, but not without leaving one brother behind in prison as collateral that they would return. The problem with pretending is that you can only do it for so long. Eventually, you will either be found out (exposed by someone else), or not be able to deal with the stress and pressure and must confess the truth. Finally, it can make you unable to live freely and end up living your life on the edge and miserable.

So how did it all turn out for Joseph? Joseph could no longer control himself. He had to come clean. He had to let go of all the past pain and hurts that his brothers had caused him and forgive them. He had a choice to make.

Read the following Scriptures and fill in the blanks.

Genesis 45:1

"Then Joseph could no longer control himself before all his attendants, and he cried out, "Have everyone leave my presence!" So, there was no one with Joseph when he made himself _____ to his brothers." (NIV)

After Joseph declared who he was, his brothers were terrified and could not speak to him. Three verses later Joseph declared again who he was to his brothers.

Genesis 45:4

"Then Joseph said to his brothers, "Come close to me." When they had done so, he said, I am your _____ the one you sold into Egypt." (NIV)

Can you hear their heart skip a beat? They must have been barely able to stand under the pressure and fear of what was going to happen to them.

Read Genesis 45:5-11 and summarize what took place.

Write out verses Genesis 45:7-8 – Who did Joseph say sent him there?

48

Read Genesis 45:14-15:

"Then he (Joseph) threw his arms around his brother Benjamin and wept, and Benjamin embraced him weeping. And he kissed all his brothers and wept over them. Afterwards the brothers talked to him." (NIV) Did you catch the word "afterwards"?

After Joseph removed the mask and was vulnerable and transparent, he showed himself. THEN healing took place. Imagine the tension in the room and then the joy that burst forth when the brothers were reunited again, but this time with no deception.

In both stories of the Patriarchs, a beautiful ending is portrayed because of forgiveness and transparency. The past was left behind, and an opportunity for new beginnings unfolded. In both situations the siblings had to let their offenses go. They had to choose to not let their past hold any power over them. They had to risk being transparent and vulnerable not knowing how the other would respond. They all came to a point of transparency which allowed them to experience a new relationship with their families, a new freedom in being who they were. All involved learned humility. All learned forgiveness.

Have you ever gone through an experience that was difficult, but when you got through it you saw that God had used it for a greater purpose for you or someone else? Write it below.

Day 3:
TRANSPARENCY IS A CHOICE AND A RISK

Cinda describes her decision "to choose consciously" to become transparent: "I made a life-changing decision right then and there. I would never again allow another person to wield power over my life. I would never again live behind a mask, pretending to be anyone other than myself. From now on I would live a life of transparency, a life of truth. By this, I would set myself free! If people liked me for who I was, great. If they did not, at the end of the day, I would still like myself."[20]

Many of us desire to be a person that is transparent and real, but "fear" stops you in your tracks, especially if you are hiding something. When you are hiding something from the world, the last thing you are thinking about is being transparent. Fear causes you to hide.

Cinda continues, "Was it scary at first? You bet. But every time I felt scared, I remembered what it felt like to constantly live-in fear of someone exposing the "real me." I remembered how much

energy it took to wear that mask of deception, and it hardened my resolve to never act that role again. I realized the new vision of my future far outweighed any fear I may experience. Eventually transparency became a habit. I stayed true to myself and therefore to others. This habit eventually became ingrained in my character and core belief system."[21]

Are you pretending to be someone you are not? It takes a lot of energy to hide the truth and keep up the charade of deception. When you cannot expose yourself to anyone else, there is someone you can talk to: God. He will accept you and love you right where you are. When you give your fear of being exposed to Jesus, He will navigate you through the deep waters to a place of calm and peace. You are safe with Him.

Queen Esther – Removes Her Mask for "Such a Time as This"

One of the famous quotes from the Bible you hear people say is, *"Who knows, maybe you were made for such a time as this."* (Esther 4:14 NIV) Let us take a closer look at this story at the beginning where Esther is at the palace preparing for her visit to the king. The king is in the process of choosing a new queen from the most beautiful women of the land. As Esther prepares, one particularly important piece of information is given to the reader.

Read Esther 2:10; 2:20 – What does it tell us that Esther did not reveal in both these scriptures?

As the story continues, King Xerxes is pleased with Esther and he selects her as the new "Queen of Persia." Mordecai, Esther's cousin who raised her, overhears two guards plotting to assassinate the King and reports it to Esther. Esther in turn tells the King, and he executes the two guards. Meanwhile, King Xerxes places Haman in a seat of honor higher than all the other nobles. Mordecai received no reward for his action that saved the King, which was customary. Keeping true to his belief, Mordecai refuses to kneel to Haman because Haman's ancestors were ancient enemies of the Jews. Haman is so enraged that Mordecai would not bow down to him, that he devises a plan to kill all the Jews. Haman approaches the King with the plot, and King Xerxes agrees to the edict. When the word gets out, Mordecai dresses himself in sackcloth and begins to mourn. Esther is told of this and sends word to Mordecai asking what is wrong. When the answer comes back to her through the eunuch that is assigned to her, she learns of the plot to kill the Jews. Mordecai encourages Esther to go to the King, but Esther is afraid for two reasons: 1) No one approaches the king unless he holds out the golden scepter to them and 2) She has a secret that she does not want out, of who she really is—a Jew. Does she risk exposing her identity to the king? Mordecai sends out one final plea to Esther.

50

Read Esther 4:10-14

What does Mordecai remind her in verse 13?

Esther tells Mordecai to have the Jews who are in Susa fast for three days and nights. When the people fast, they are also praying for God's intervention. After three days Esther prepares to go to the king where she will beseech the king on her people's behalf, thus exposing who she really is.

Read Chapter 7:3-5 and describe what Esther says.

How did King Xerxes respond? (verse 7:5-7)

In the end, Esther saves her people from annihilation. When she approaches the king and reveals who she really is, the king has favor on her and acts upon her request. Esther is vulnerable and transparent, and the king responds to her favorably.

There was no longer any more hidden identities. I wonder how their relationship changed after this incident. Transparency and vulnerability were critical for Esther to accomplish what God wanted to do through her. Are you willing to allow God to use you in ways that require transparency and vulnerability?

Day 4:
A NEW CREATION – GOD'S PATIENT PROCESS

When you accepted Jesus, He wiped out your past and made you a "new creation." The enemy would try to convince you that you are not a new creation by using fear, especially fear of what others know. Some of you who are reading this may be thinking, "But I keep falling back into old habits even though I am already a Christian." God is a God of infinite grace. He knows that the enemy is constantly tempting and attacking you in the areas that you are weakest, and yes, sometimes you fall again, but even when you fall, Jesus stays with you. He is right there. The good news is that God is still in the process of changing you.

When the Holy Spirit dwells in you, you probably felt the presence of God even in the midst of sinning. You heard the Holy Spirit whisper to you, calling you back. God does not leave you when you fall back into sin. He is faithful to remain with you. He is focused on drawing you back, and you have not blown your last chance. He has not given up on you. Yes, He wants you to move beyond temptation and falling into sin, but if (and when) you do fall, He is there to walk through it with you. You are no longer the person you were, but there is refining that still needs to be done. This process is called sanctification and is the process God uses to make you more like Him.

> *"And we all, who with unveiled faces contemplate the Lord's glory, are being transformed into his image with ever-increasing glory, which comes from the Lord, who is the Spirit."*
> *2 Corinthians 3:18 (NIV)*

What do these Scriptures say about being a new creation in Jesus?

Isaiah 43:18

Ezekiel 11:19

Ezekiel 36:26

Ephesians 4:23-24

Colossians 3:7-10

2 Corinthians 5:17

2 Corinthians 3:15-18

Becoming a new creation does not happen overnight. It is often a process of walking through the fire, but it is in the fire we are changed. He will continue to change you and purify your heart, and each day you walk with Him, you will be a little more like Him.

In the Beth Moore Bible Study, "Here and Now…There and Then, A Lecture Series of Revelation," she talks about how "God doesn't make all new things but makes all things new." He does not start from scratch and eliminate your past as if it never happened, but he takes you where you are and "makes you a new creation."[22] You are not the same person you were. Your past is the testimony of the faithfulness of God rescuing you out of the pit and taking you and making you a "new creation." Your freedom is only a prayer away. So, take heart; there are good things coming.

Healing Starts With Vulnerability and Transparency

Healing starts at the place of vulnerability. Start with just determining to be open and vulnerable toward God. He is perfectly safe to talk to, especially since He knows you better than you know yourself. Once you have experienced the beauty of vulnerability, you can see why it is critical to healing, freedom and developing authentic relationships. He has a tender side, a side that welcomes you into an intimate place to share deeply, that offers acceptance, honesty, and safety in a way that can be life changing to others and you.

Choosing who to be vulnerable with is a process. As you begin to see the freedom that living in the truth brings, you will naturally begin to open up to others. You may have a small core group of people you feel safe with, so be open to those people God places before you and seek Him with how vulnerable He wants you to be. Remember being deceitful is never right in God's eyes. Strive to be truthful and honest with everyone, but always do so with an attitude of love and genuine concern.

Being in God's Presence Changes Us

When we spend time in God's presence, we cannot help but be changed. The way we interact with others will be impacted whether we are aware of it or not. God chose Moses to deliver his people, the Israelites, from bondage. From the first encounter, where God appeared to Moses in the burning bush through the rest of Moses' days, Moses sought the presence of God daily. Spending time in the presence of God was Moses' lifestyle.

Read Exodus 34:29-34.

What physical change did the people see on Moses?

Why was Moses' face radiant?

Relook at verse 34 again. What did Moses do whenever he entered the Lord's presence to speak with Him?

Moses removed the veil over his face when He came before God. There was nothing blocking his face from the Lord. In Moses' transparency, God's radiance came upon his face. When Moses came down the mountain, the people could not even look at Him because his face was so radiant. When you are spending time in God's presence, people will notice a difference in your countenance. You cannot be in God's presence and not be changed.

Day 5:
MINISTERING TO OTHERS

When others are ministering to us, or we are ministering to others, we must be willing to share things we have gone through to allow someone else (or us) to find freedom. God uses those things in our past that we have walked through. You do not have to stand up and shout it to the world, but when God brings someone to you that is going through something you went through, are you willing to be vulnerable and share your experience to help them gain freedom? The same is true when you are being ministered to. When you are open and honest, it opens the door to freedom.

When we share openly with those God has sent to us, we give permission to others to also open up. Honesty and openness prepare a safe place for others to enter. Walls come down with transparency and vulnerability. When we share our painful experiences and how God has used them to heal us or help us grow in our character and walk, it gives others hope that the same will happen for them. When hearts are open, honest, and tender, much can be accomplished for others which brings great glory to the Father. A word of warning – vulnerability does not allow you to expose and harm another person. We have the right to be open and honest about our own lives, but we do not have the right to expose details about another's life without their permission. Sharing and being honest is critical to bringing healing, but always honor other people's privacy.

Are you willing to become more vulnerable? To live a life of honesty and truth?

Examine your heart honestly. In what areas do you need to allow God to remove your masks and to make you more transparent and vulnerable so you can heal and help others to heal?

God Is the Giver of Justice – He Is the One Who Avenges You

In her book, Cinda shared about how her husband used the example of Nabal to work through some exceedingly difficult emotions. The story of Nabal brings forth a critical point for all of us to hold onto: God is the one who serves justice, and He will be faithful on our behalf to do what He feels is just.

Please read the Story of Nabal in 1 Samuel 25:26

The story of Nabal is often overlooked in Scripture, yet it has an especially important message for us today. When we are treated unfairly in our life, it is easy to want to seek revenge or get justice. We pass judgment on others, and we tend to think we know what they deserve for the consequences of their actions.

Write a summary of what was happening to David.

Reread 1 Samuel 25:30-31 – What good advice did Abigail give David?

How did David respond to Abigail in 1 Samuel 25:32?

What happened to Nabal? 1 Samuel 25:36-38

David had every right to want revenge on Nabal, but it is never the Lord's heart for us to seek revenge. "Do not seek revenge in your own hand, it is evil in the Lord's sight." God avenged, not David. God took Nabal's life – justice was served.

> *"So, when David heard that Nabal was dead, he said, "Blessed be the LORD, who has avenged the insult I received at the hand of Nabal and has kept back his servant from evil; the Lord has returned the evil doing of Nabal upon his own head. 1 Samuel 25:39 (RSV)*

What do the following Scriptures teach us about judgment and revenge?

Psalm 136:14

Ezekiel 26:14 – What did Edom become because they took revenge?

Jeremiah 51:6

Jeremiah 51:56

You cannot go through life without someone eventually hurting you. Instead of seeking revenge, we are to align ourselves with the Word of God and seek His counsel to change our heart. It is not our job to deliver justice, it is God's. He has a better plan.

Ask God to show you anyone that you need to surrender to Him.

Is there unforgiveness toward another person that has power over your life?

Write down the names of those people you need to forgive.

Take a few minutes seeking forgiveness from the Father. You may want to say a prayer like this: "Father, I choose to forgive _____ . I repent of my unforgiveness toward _____ . Lord, open my eyes to how you see _____ . Take my unforgiveness and exchange it for your heart toward _____ . Help me to walk in love. In Jesus name I pray, amen."

Now, ask the Father if there is anything He wants you to do in response to your releasing unforgiveness. If He speaks to you, obey His voice. If you do not hear any directions, enjoy your newfound freedom!

56

God wants you to be the person He created you to be. Your identity is based upon not what you do, but who you are. You are a child of the living God. The Creator of the universe chose to create you. He thought about you, pondered over you, and then created you. There were no mistakes in how He made you. He does not want you to pretend to be someone you are not. He wants you to be who He created you to be. Take off the mask of hypocrisy you may be wearing and just be you. Be real with God. Share with Him your struggles, frustrations, fears, and emotions. Share your heart – He will be faithful to meet your needs. He already knows what you need. He is just waiting for you to come to Him. He is willing and ready to meet all your needs according to His good and perfect will.

It is time to make sure your closet is clean. If you have realized that you have not been walking in vulnerability, begin by confessing your sin to the Father who is rich in mercy and unfailing in love. He will be faithful to forgive you. Ask the Father to gently begin removing your masks, and, as He does, be obedient to what He tells you to do. Remember, God wants you free. You can trust Him.

Prayer for Choosing to Remove the Mask
By Cinda Gregory

"Heavenly Father, when Jesus walked this earth, He modeled transparency and vulnerability for all to see. He was able to relate to others freely and openly. Father, that is the desire of my heart. I want the freedom and confidence to be true to myself. To be comfortable with who I really am. I am so tired of trying to perform to please others. I am so tired of pretending to be someone other than who I am. I see the blessings of transparency and vulnerability, and I want it to be part of my life. Father, I ask that You would first deal with the fear. I admit that the thought of being fully transparent and vulnerable is scary. Right now, Father, I choose to break the fear of man off my life. I admit that I have been more concerned with pleasing people than pleasing You. I repent of that and I ask your forgiveness. Thank you, Father, that by the blood of Jesus I am washed whiter than snow. Your Word says that perfect love casts out all fear, so right now I ask that where fear once gripped my heart that You would now come and fill me with Your perfect love. Thank you, Father for Your tangible love. As I quiet myself before You, would you speak to me? Would You share Your heart with me and tell me what You think of me? How special I am to You? Thank you, Daddy. Abba, I ask that You now give me courage to deal with anything that I have hidden in my closet. I no longer want to live with the skeletons of my past controlling my life and causing me to live in fear. I want to walk in freedom, so I give You permission to search it out. I choose to deal with every item that you show me. Show me, Father. I come into agreement with You that this will no longer have any power over my life. I choose to bring it OUT of

the closet into your Glorious Light and will deal with it as you direct. All power that it once had; I now break off by the power of the blood of Jesus. Thank you!

Now, Father, I choose to come into agreement with You and Your Word. Your Word says, "Who the Son sets free is free indeed." I thank You for that. I choose to walk in that freedom. I choose to genuinely love and help others instead of being afraid of them. No longer will I be afraid of what they might think of me. I choose to only fear You, God; to love what you love and hate what You hate. You and You alone will I fear. You will be my guide; You will be my standard. I will walk in your love. Amaze me God, with the freedom that will come into my life from these decisions. Let it bring freedom not just to my life, but also to all those that I come into contact with. Amen." [23]

Week 4:
Leaving Chance Behind –
Choosing to Be Intentional

Key #4 – Intentional Growth Is a Choice

Day 1:
GOD IS INTENTIONAL

Morning people – I am not one of them. My husband is. Going to the gym at 5:30 AM on a blustery winter day does not bother him one bit. As he is getting his blood pumping, I am burying myself deeper into my covers to catch just a few more minutes of sleep. But once my feet hit the floor, I am on the move all day till I am ready to go to bed once again.

How do you wake up? Are you ready to jump into the new day with an expectant attitude toward what the day will bring? Are you excited to live your life and ready to engage all that this day will bring your way? We have choices on how we will react to situations that face each day. Life should not just happen to us. The secret to living the abundant life (or life to the fullest) is to live with "intentionality".

Recently, wherever I go, I keep hearing the words "being intentional." One of my favorite people is Joanna Gaines from the show "Fixer Upper" on HGTV. On the cover of the Magnolia Journal, Issue 6 (Spring 2018) Intentional Living were the words, "Taking a Look at Intentional Living."[24] So, what is the big deal with being intentional? If we are not intentional about our lives, society will dictate for us what we should be doing, watching, learning, wearing, eating, how to raise our children, etc. Being intentional means you are purposeful in your word and action. You think about the choices you make. You live each day to the fullest, focusing on what is truly important to you.

On the quest to becoming more intentional, we must be careful to guard our dreams, those things that God has put in us. We need to be intentional with what we do or do not allow in our lives. Being intentional begins with us knowing our purpose and goals and going after them with determination, boldness, and an unwavering focus.

God Is Intentional

From the beginning of time we see a God that is "intentional". God planned things with great care and intentionality. From Genesis to Revelation, we see God's heart riveted on one thing – His children and having a relationship with them. Before you were born, God had a plan for you.

Read the Scriptures below and write down the main points of each Scripture.

"Before I formed you in the womb I knew you, before you were born I set you apart; I appointed you as prophet to the nations." Jeremiah 1:5 (NIV)

1)

2)

3)

"For I know the plans I have for you, declares the Lord, "plans to prosper you and not harm you, plans to give you a hope and future."" Jeremiah 29:11 (NIV)

1)

2)

3)

"For you created my inmost being; you knit me together in my mother's womb. I praise you because I am fearfully and wonderfully made; your works are wonderful, I know that full well. My frame was not hidden from you when I was made in the secret place. When I was woven together in the depths of the earth, your eyes saw my unformed body. All the days ordained for me were written in your book before one of them came to be." Psalm 139:13-16 (NIV)

1)

2)

3)

These Scriptures point to one thing: you were planned and created "intentionally" by God. He wants you to achieve the purpose that He has planned for you and created you for. God wants you to be purposeful in your decisions, how you live and act.

When you make choices, take time to think them through. Will my choice allow me to move forward toward fulfilling the calling that God has for my life? Are you being intentional about the direction your life is taking? Are you leaving too much to chance, just taking one day at a time and not thinking about where you are headed? Are there areas in your life in which you should be planning and practicing self-discipline? So often we are not doing anything wrong or heading in a bad direction; we just are not being intentional.

Personal Growth Requires Intentionality

Anything that you want to accomplish takes planning to make it a reality. Begin to focus on what you feel is important in your life. Ask God what His dreams and goals are for you. Write them down and begin to determine how you can begin to live more intentionally to accomplish those things God has set before you. It is time to start living intentionally. Below are several areas we will call "traps" that the enemy sets up, and if we buy into them, will derail us from living intentionally and accomplishing God's purpose.

In the book, Intentional Living: Choosing a Life That Matters, John Maxwell writes: "If I wanted to make a difference … Wishing for things to change wouldn't make them change. Hoping for improvements would not bring them. Dreaming would not provide all the answers I needed. Vision would not be enough to bring transformation to me or to others. Only by managing my thinking and shifting my thoughts from desire to deeds would I be able to bring about positive change. I needed to go from wanting to, to doing."[25]

Day 2:
CLEAN UP YOUR HOUSE!

Get Rid of the Traps the Enemy Sets for You So You Can Move Forward

Before you can focus your attention on living an intentional life, there may be a little cleaning that needs to be done. Not everyone likes to clean house, but our spiritual house needs to be cleaned out from time to time to allow us to move forward into our destiny. Below are several areas, or traps, that can keep us from having freedom and living an intentional life.

 **Trap #1: The Past – To Move Forward, You Need "To Let Go of the Past"**

Read the following Scriptures and complete the blanks:

Isaiah 43:18-19:

"Forget the _____ things; do not dwell on the past. See, I am doing a _____ thing! Now it springs up; do you not perceive it? I am making a way in the desert and streams in the wasteland." (NIV)

Philippians 3:12-14:

"Not that I have already obtained all this, or have already arrived at my goal, but I press on to take hold of that for which Christ Jesus took hold of me. Brothers and sisters, I do not consider myself yet to have taken hold of it. But one thing I do: _____ what is behind and straining toward what is ahead, I press on _____ the goal to _____ the prize for which God has called me heavenward in Christ Jesus." (NIV)

The past is the past; let it go.

 **Trap #2: Unforgiveness – Forgiving Those Who Have Hurt or Offended You**

It is critical for you to forgive those people from whom you are withholding forgiveness. Unforgiveness keeps you enslaved to other people and gives them power over you. Failure to forgive blocks the flow of God moving in your life. It is important to remember that forgiveness is "a choice," not "a feeling." You have to choose to forgive, sometimes over and over in a single day. Through the repetition of speaking forgiveness, you will begin to feel a wonderful sense of freedom. God has a lot to say in His Scripture about forgiveness, and He is clear what He expects of His followers.

Complete the blanks in the Scriptures below.

Matthew 6:14-15:

"For if you _____ other people when they sin against you, your heavenly Father will also _____ you. But if you do not _____ others their sins, your Father will not forgive your sins." (NIV)

Matthew 18:21-22:

"Then Peter came to Jesus and asked, "Lord, how _____ times shall I _____ my brother or sister who sins against me? Up to seven times? Jesus answered, "I tell you, not seven times, but seventy-seven _____ ." (NIV)

Mark 11:25:

"And when you stand praying, if you hold anything against anyone, _____ , so that your Father in heaven _____ your sins." (NIV)

Ephesians 4:32:

"Be kind and compassionate to one another, _____ each other, just as in Christ God _____ you." (NIV)

One last thought on which to meditate. Do I hold any offenses against God? We often know when we are offended by people, but how often are we upset, annoyed and frustrated with God over a situation? Do we take up an offense against God especially when we see other people receive the healing we or a loved one needs, or someone else gets the promotion that we deserved, or watching others seem to sail through life, and we go through one struggle after another?

Please fill in the missing word in the blank below.

Matthew 11:6 states:

"And blessed is he who is not _____ because of me." (NKJV)

It is critical to acknowledge if we are harboring an offense toward God and ask Him to forgive us for holding that offense, then repent and fill that place that once held the offense with the faithfulness of God. Focus on how He has loved you, over and over, even when you were offensive to Him!

Pray – Ask God to show any offenses you may have toward others or Him. Repent and seek forgiveness for anything He shows you. Now, enjoy the freedom you have just received!

 ### Trap #3: Fear – The Fear Trap Is One of Satan's Favorites Because It Immobilizes Us From Moving Forward

After I started drawing closer to God, He began to deal with the fear inside of me. Basically, I was a very fearful, insecure person, because I learned at an early age people could not be trusted. My default pattern was fear. When things looked difficult, I would fear I could not do it. When I needed to step out and meet new people, fear of rejection flooded in. When I felt threatened or not good enough, fear reared its ugly head as control and manipulation. When I wanted to try something new, fear of failure stopped me from stepping out and trying. The fear of failure was greater than my desire to take the risk. God began revealing to me that my fear and insecurity was rooted in not trusting Him. Though fear and insecurity are an enormously powerful stronghold to overcome, God assured me that He is the ultimate power, that He could make the impossible possible. It was simply a matter of trusting Him. Faith is believing that God will protect me. Fear was believing He would not.

I would find fear and insecurity creeping in when I felt I had let God down. I would become convinced that God was mad at me and that He was just waiting to punish me. The idea that God would wipe out my past sins as if they never happened seemed beyond my comprehension. When your brain is trained to think a certain way, it can take a while to retrain your thought patterns. Reading the Scriptures and memorizing them helped. I needed to take seriously 2 Corinthians 10:5 which told me to take every thought captive and make it obedient to Christ. I would say to myself over and over the words from 2 Timothy 1:7 (KJV) – "For God hath not given us the spirit of fear; but of power, and love, and of a sound mind." Believing it was a whole different matter.

God's Holy Spirit gives us power, love, and a sound, disciplined mind, which is the opposite of fear and panic. I needed to renew my mind. I needed to take on the mind of Christ. If God is for me, who can stand against me? I needed to train myself to think positively and not dwell on what may or may not happen. In the book of Matthew 6:25-34, we are told to not worry about tomorrow, put our trust in God, and do not try and work things out in our own mind. God knows the end from the beginning.

"Fear not" is the most repeated command in the Scriptures. God consistently tells us to not be afraid or fearful. Fear is a default reaction that we fall into when we are in situations that we cannot control or see a way out or when we think about unknown things in the future. When we give our fears, insecurities, and worries over to God, we begin to allow God's divine plan for our lives to unfold. We start walking in faith and trust that "He works all things together for the good for those who love him." (Romans 8:28 NIV) God has called us to be significant. Do not let fear or insecurity rob you of your call nor your destiny.

Please read the story of Ahaz the King of Judah in Isaiah Chapter 7.

What situation was unfolding in this chapter?

What were the things God told Ahaz through the prophet Isaiah?

1.

2.

3.

4.

5.

6.

Which one of the six statements is the most difficult for you to walk in?

Which one of the six statements is the easiest for you to walk in?

God was calling King Ahaz to trust Him. He sent the prophet Isaiah to him to give the King Godly advice. Unfortunately, King Ahaz did not listen to Isaiah. The wise advice Isaiah gave the king is appropriate advice for us as well. When in a crisis God wants us to: be careful (be wise), keep calm, do not be afraid, do not lose heart. Most of the things we worry about will not happen, but if they do, God will fight for you. Stand firm in your faith, otherwise you most assuredly will fall. Next time you are in a crisis, remind yourself of these six commands God spoke to Ahaz through Isaiah.

God commands us over and over, "Do not Fear," "Do not be afraid." The only way to do this is to fill our minds with Scripture and meditate on it. The Scriptures we repeat over and over become the weapons with which we fight the enemy. Reading and meditating on Scripture can be the difference between making good versus poor decisions, which can make your life unbearable.

Below are some Scriptures that can breathe life into you when walking through times of difficulty:

Isaiah 41:10:

"So do not fear, for I am with you; do not be _____ , for I am your God; I will _____ you and _____ you; I will _____ with my righteous right hand." (NIV)

Isaiah 41:13:

"For I am the Lord, your God, who takes hold of your right hand; and says to you, Do _____ ; I will _____ you." (NIV)

Joshua 1:9:

"Have not I commanded you? Be _____ and _____ . Do not be _____ ; do not be discouraged, for the Lord your God will be with you wherever you go." (NIV)

Deuteronomy 3:22:

"Do not be _____ of them; the Lord your God himself will _____ for you." (NIV)

Deuteronomy 31:8:

"The Lord himself goes before you and will be with you; he will _____ leave you nor forsake you. Do not be _____ ; do not be discouraged." (NIV)

2 Timothy 1:7:

"For God has not given us a spirit of _____ and timidity, but of _____ , _____ , and _____ ." (NLT)

John 14:27:

"Peace I leave with you; my _____ I give you. I do not give to you as the world gives. Do _____ let your hearts be troubled and do _____ be afraid." (NIV)

Creating an intentional life requires that we stop responding with our emotions and start walking in the truth. When we believe God's Word and His promises over us, and apply them to all our circumstances, we begin living our life the way it was meant to be lived – fearlessly.

 **Trap #4:**
Comparison

> *"The moment you move into comparison is the moment you*
> *disconnect from your identity."* (Author Unknown)

Few things in walking out our call or destiny with intentionality will trip us up more than comparing ourselves to others. God does not want us comparing our walk to someone else's walk. Your walk is unique to you; it should not look like anyone else's. Past experiences of being cast aside, devalued, or not noticed can cause people to feel rejected, which can blossom into insecurity and at its worst, self-hatred. When we embrace self-hatred, fear of failure, rejection and thoughts of not being worthy of success, we are immobilized from stepping out intentionally in just about every area of our lives.

Read John 21:20-23 – What was going on between Peter and Jesus?

What does Peter ask the Lord about him?

What was Jesus' reply?

What does that speak to you?

Read 2 Corinthians 10:12 and write the warning Paul spoke.

Insecurity is often rooted in pride. In this Scripture above, Paul was talking to the Pharisees who often tried to prove their goodness by comparing themselves with others, rather than with God's standards. This is dangerous thinking. Comparing ourselves to others can cause us to think that we are not that bad after all, "Look at what they are doing; I don't do that." We therefore justify sin in our lives. Comparison can bring a sense of false pride when that comparison makes us feel good about ourselves. Comparison can also bring devastation when we compare and see that we are not as good as others. Thoughts like: I am not as smart, not as good looking, not as talented, not as good a parent, my family isn't perfect like…, and the list goes on. When we measure ourselves by God's standards, none of us have basis for pride. Our focus should be - how is my life aligning up to what God wants it to be? How can my life be more like Jesus' life? How can I be more like Him? We were meant to be companions, not competitors. Christ's directive is for us to "follow Him." Our eyes should be on Him, not others.

 ## Trap #5:
Not Enough Time – The Secret Place

We are too busy. We are way too stressed and exhausted. Our society has impacted us so that we seem to be running here and there, and we find ourselves feeling overwhelmed, depressed, and even guilty. God is calling us into the secret place where we can be renewed and refreshed in His presence.

When you were little, did you have a secret hiding place or a place you went to be alone? My secret place was the "crawl space" in the basement of our house. It was a short room, elevated above the floor that was sand. When I reflect back, I can't believe that dirty, dark place was where I would go to escape. It was out of the way and no one ever came there. I was alone with my thoughts. God is calling you into the secret place, a place of rest where He can spend time with just you. It is when you spend this quiet time with God that you will hear His voice most clearly. Peace and rest come when we enter the place of rest, in God's presence, where God pours out His love, His revelation, His power and authority into you. It strengthens you. Discover your secret place. Make it a place where you are comfortable, where you feel relaxed and peaceful.

When I lived in Colorado, there was a mountain in the foothills called Cheyenne Mountain which contained "NORAD", an underground government strategic headquarters. It was always intriguing to think about what important things were happening inside that mountain. Our secret place is like that, a place where God reveals His divine strategies. We need strategies in how to defeat the enemy, how to handle relationships, how to minister to the lost. Heidi Baker said in one of her devotion books, "There are no short-cuts to the anointing." The anointing comes by spending time in God's presence in the secret place. If we do not take the time in the secret place (quiet time), we will not reach all that God has planned for us. Jesus had a place, the Mount of Olives, where He retreated often to spend time talking and praying to His Father. If it was important for Jesus to spend time alone with God, it is even more important for us to do so.

Our society has not trained us to value quiet time. It often feels uncomfortable when we are "forcing ourselves" to have quiet time. God does not want guilt to be the motivating factor to spending time with Him. We need to retrain our mind to value this time. When I began to work on having a consistent quiet time, I started out with a short devotion book (Sarah Young's, Jesus Calling).[26] It did not take long to read, and I found that I was enjoying the time reading Scripture. I would often put on a worship song before I began reading to help me block out the world and draw myself into God's presence. Find whatever works for you to calm your spirit before you begin your time with the Father. As you embark on increasing your time alone with God, have grace for yourself. If you miss a day, a week, or even more, begin again. Remember no change will happen unless you make it happen.

Time alone with God always has a way of helping you refocus on what is important. Try to find some undistracted time every day just to spend with God. A few minutes in the presence of the Father can help you accomplish so much more than when you rush into the day without giving it to Him. Do not forget to allow Him into your plans.

Trap #6:
Declaring Myself Not Useful Because of My Past

For some people their journey has been so difficult, their past so littered with sin, that they cannot begin to imagine being useful to God. Scripture is full of people that one would think would never be useful to God. Let us look at a few of these people.

68

Rahab – From Prostitute to Child of God
Please read the story of Rahab in Joshua 2:1-24.

What was Rahab's profession?

What did Rahab do?

Why did Rahab hide the spies? (Verses 8-12)

What was Rahab's reward?

Read Hebrews 11:31 – What was her ultimate reward?

Rahab risked everything she had for a God she barely knew. She did not allow her past to keep her from the new role God had for her. She listened to the still small whisper inside and chose to take a risk that changed her life forever.

Saul (Paul) – From Persecutor to Proclaimer
Please read the story of Saul (Paul) in Acts: 7:54-60; Acts 8:1-3.

When we first meet Saul what was he doing? What was his goal?

In Acts 9:1-16, what was God's plan for Saul?

Read Philippians 2:13:

> *"For it is God who works in you to will and to act according to his good purpose." (NIV)*

What work is God doing in you? God is directing your path. At key places in your life, He turns you around and points you in a different direction. Sometimes He does this through circumstances, a crisis, or by drawing you to study His Word. God gives you a "wake up call" and redirects your path from where you were headed. As we walk with God, He does the "work" in us. Work means just that, work. It does not happen overnight. To accomplish our destiny, it takes intentional work in our lives.

Am I declaring myself not useful because of my past? If so, take a few minutes and seek God's forgiveness and repent to God those areas that you have allowed your past to keep you from what God has for you.

Day 3:
YOU HAVE TO HAVE A FAITH VISION

In Strong's Concordance, faith is described as "assured, convinced, persuaded; or trust (in God)."[27] Faith and vision go hand in hand.

> *"For with the heart one believes unto righteousness, and with the mouth confession is made until salvation." Romans 10:10 (New King James)*

Similar to the Scripture above, one must believe it in the heart first and then confess it. It is the same with "vision". You must believe in your heart what God has placed in you and then speak forth the vision with faith. For our lives to conform to God's plan, we must be able to see things as God sees them. Often, we are far from what God says we should be. That is when faith becomes important.

Read the following Scriptures and answer the questions.

Proverbs 29:18 – What does this say about vision?

Philippians 2:13 – Who does the work in you? And why?

Habakkuk 2:2-3 – What do we have to do?

Proverbs 21:5 – What do our plans lead to?

2 Chronicles 15:7 – What does this verse encourage us to do?

Vision gives life. God has a faith vision for each one of us. Sometimes we get a glimpse of it, but may disregard it, because our lives do not resemble it. We cannot imagine how we are going to get from where we are to where God has spoken for us to be. When we know what God has spoken and promised to us, and we have the faith to agree with God, we begin to receive life from His vision. God is waiting for us to line up with His will and agree with His vision for us. When we do, we will bring God's will to pass here on earth.

Determining Your Priorities

Ask yourself these three questions:

> **1. What do I spend my money on?**
>
> **2. What do I spend my time thinking about?**
>
> **3. What do I spend my time doing?**

The answer to these questions will often point to the very thing that is a "priority" in your life. Priorities are things that we tend to be very "intentional" about achieving. No matter how busy we are, we always seem to find time for our priorities. We should have priorities in our lives, but they should line up with the vision God has for us.

How do your priorities measure up to your vision or purpose?

Seek God and watch how He is using you in your life right now. Do you know what God's purpose is for your life? What goals and dreams have been planted in your heart? What are the things that you do well and seem to come naturally to you? (If you do not know, ask someone close to you; they will probably see it more clearly than you do.) Look back over your life. Are there things that seem to go together, or line up, moving you in a certain direction? Have doors of unexpected opportunity opened for you that seem to fall in line with those dreams that stir in your heart? Ask God to bring revelation to what His purpose and plan is for you. God is not trying to hide it from you – ask Him.

What are the things that stir in your heart?

What do you dream of?

What are your goals? (Are they man-made or God-made goals?)

What do you believe is God's vision for you? Who were you meant to be?

Principle to Live By: *"If you want to have great impact be intentional."* [28] **(John Maxwell)**

I once heard someone say, "No decision is a decision to do nothing." Change starts with a decision. Plans start with a decision. Do not sit and wait until you have created what you think is a perfect plan, because in the days and months of planning you may have missed some of the opportunities God had planned for you. Do not delay. Do not let fear, anxiety, or feelings of inadequacy rob you of your dream and purpose. It is time to take a step; you start by "beginning". Remember you are not doing this alone. God, who already has the plan, is guiding your path as you begin the journey toward your purpose and vision.

A good way to begin to train yourself in being more intentional is to make a list. Pray and ask God to direct you as you begin listing things that you believe are important for you to do to bring you closer to your vision. Review your list, set some goals you want to achieve, and how you plan to achieve them. Set a timeline for yourself for each goal you want to accomplish. Be realistic. What can I do this week, this month, this year and so on.

Begin by first doing something small, then when you succeed, do something else. Be consistent in your decisions, choosing to do things that move you in a forward direction toward your goal. Make all of your decisions and choices through the backdrop of your vision. Ask God to help you evaluate how you are doing on accomplishing the goals you have set together. Ask yourself, "Is this moving me closer to my goal or away from it?" There may be some things in your life that are not productive in moving you toward your vision. Remove those things that are stumbling blocks in reaching your vision. This is living your life intentionally.

What areas of your life need to be pruned and adjusted to achieve your dreams/goals?

What steps can you take to help move forward toward achieving your vision?

Your purpose is the race set before you. Your race has been planned since the beginning of time. No one else's race looks like yours, so stop comparing your calling with others and begin running the race God intended for you.

Read: Philippians 3:14: – What do you have to do to win the race or the prize?

Day 4:
GUIDELINES FOR BEING INTENTIONAL

The Apostle Paul gives us some practical guidelines to help us be more intentional in our living.

Read Colossians 4:2-6 and complete the four guidelines that Paul states on living your life intentionally, therefore having a greater impact for the Kingdom of God.

🎯 1. Be intentional in what you _____. (Colossians 4:3-4)

What do the following Scriptures say about prayer?

Matthew 7:7

Matthew 16:19

Ephesians 3:20

Philippians 4:6

Colossians 4:2

Hebrews 4:16

James 4:2

1 John 5:14

🎯 **2. Be intentional in how you _____ toward people. (Colossians 4:5)**

We are to look for people to engage with and share the gospel. I have always liked the saying, "Make a friend, be a friend, lead a friend to Christ." It is often our actions, how we treat people, that will draw people to us. Once people see we care about them, they will be more likely to listen to what we have to say. Serving others. Loving others. Putting others first. These actions will draw others to the Father through you. Be intentional (and sincere) in how you act toward others.

Fill in the blanks with the appropriate words.

Ephesians 5:15-16

"Be very careful, then, how you live, not as unwise but as wise, making the _____ of every _____ , because the days are evil. Therefore, do not be foolish but understand what the Lord's will is." (NIV)

Colossians 4:5

"Be wise in the way you act toward outsiders; make the _____ of every _____ ." (NIV)

What similar phrases do both above Scripture's use?

Days, weeks, months, and years go by so quickly. We often hear the phrase "time flies by." There is no time to waste. The Apostle Paul encourages us to always be looking for ways and opportunities to lead others to Christ.

🎯 **3. Be intentional in what you _____ . (Colossians 4:6)**

Complete the following scriptures on choosing our words carefully.

Colossians 4:6

"Let your _____ always be full of grace, seasoned with salt, so that you may know how to answer everyone." (NIV)

James 5:12

"But above all, my brothers, do not swear, not by heaven or by earth or by any other oath, but let your "yes" be _____ , and your "no," be _____ , so that you may not fall under condemnation." (ESV)

Ephesians 4:29

"Do not let any _____ talk come out of your mouths, but only what is _____ for building others up according to their needs, that it may _____ those who listen." (NIV)

When we are in an attitude of prayer over all aspects of our lives, we will find that the way we relate to others will change significantly. We will desire our words to be engaging and inviting to people. Our words should be gracious and encouraging. We should give others our complete attention, so that they know we care about them and are engaged in that relationship. In our society, relationships are damaged by all our distractions and not being "fully present" when people are talking with us.

4. Be intentional with your _____. (Colossians 4:5)

Busyness – "the illusion that we are accomplishing something" (unknown author). We are so busy running around and packing our schedules so tight that we do not have time to do the things that are important. I heard this statement once, and it is worth meditating on, "There is a difference between being busy or being on a mission." (Author unknown) Is our busyness drawing us closer to what matters most to us, or is it a distraction?

Read the story of Martha and Mary in Luke 10:38-42.

The story opens with Jesus on His way to the home of Martha where her sister Mary and Lazarus were also awaiting His arrival.

After arriving at Martha's house what was Mary doing? What was Martha doing?

What word was used to describe Martha's attitude? (Verse 40- 41)

What complaint did Martha bring to Jesus? What did she want Jesus to do?

Write below what Jesus told Martha.

Reflection: What things in my life have been distractions from sitting at the feet of Jesus?

The enemy of our soul knows that if he can keep us focused on the world and busy chasing things that we think we need, we will run ourselves to exhaustion. Jesus reminded Martha in the text above, "Only one thing is needed."

What do the following Scriptures tell us to do?

Psalms 46:10

Psalms 37:7

Psalms 39:6

Matthew 6:33

Colossians 3:23

Jesus shared the importance of taking time to be still and just sit in the presence of God. The Word shows us that God desires us to be well-rested and in a state of peace.

What do the following Scriptures say about rest and peace?

Genesis 2:2-3

Psalms 127:2

Leviticus 23:3

Matthew 11:28-30

Mark 2:27

John 14:27

Philippians 4:6-7

Ephesians 2:8 – What three words clearly tell us that we cannot earn salvation? How does that relate to being "busy"?

When you are rested, you can think more clearly, which means you can get more done. God does not want you exhausted. Our society has us on a hamster wheel going around and around at such speed we do not even know how to rest when we have the opportunity. God created the Sabbath as a day of rest; He obviously thinks it is important. There is nothing that you have to do to earn God's favor or salvation. It is a free gift that we do not have to work for, so you can stop working yourself to exhaustion and allow yourself time to rest. Being rested will bring greater focus and accomplishment to your life. Enjoy the rest God wants to give you.

Day 5:
CHOOSE CAREFULLY WHO YOU HANG AROUND

It sounds easy to do, but in reality, it can be very difficult. It is easy to fall into relationships in the different circles of which we are a part. Work, church, school, clubs, exercise groups, etc. God calls us to not only live intentionally to obtain our goals, purposes and dreams, but He also warns us to be careful who we choose to spend our time with.

Read: 1 Corinthians 15:33 – Write it below:

It is true, you will become like those with whom you hang around. Often it is a subtle change, you may not even realize it. Either you will influence them, or they will influence you. Someone is always going to have a greater impact. Do not fool yourself thinking that you are strong enough not to be influenced. The more time you spend with someone, the greater the influence they will have on you. Surround yourself with people that have similar interests or people who encourage you and spur you on to be better. Choose people that bring life to you and do not drain you dry. Our closest friends are the ones we spend the most time with and we seek advice from. They do influence your life, whether you intend them to or not.

John Maxwell stated in one of his leadership conferences that He could reliably predict what a person's life would look like in five years simply by observing the people they spend their time with, the movies they watched and the books they read. Are you intentional with what you are putting into yourself?

Your Friends Are Influencers

Friends can determine the path of your future. Whatever age you are, the influence of peers and friends is crucial in determining where you are headed in life. You may rationalize that friends are not influencing your future in any way, but who do we spend the most time with and seek advice from? Our closest friends. They do influence our lives and help chart our future whether we intend them to or not.

Reflect on the questions below and write your thoughts.

Who are the people you admire and look up to?

78

Are there people with characteristics in them that you would like to have?

Who are people that believe the same core values that you have?

Are there people in your life who have negative influences on you?

Intentionally Choose Your Influencers

Take time now to ask God to place friends in your life that will be a good influence, that will encourage you and help you grow. People that believe the same things that you believe and are walking those beliefs out in their daily life. Ask God to readjust relationships that may be negative in your life or help you to put a healthy distance between you and them. Limit the time you spend with people who are not helping you move toward your goals. Keep loving your old friends with more limited time, so that they are no longer major influencers in your life. Surround yourself with people who think "big" and believe "all things are possible with God." Big thinkers achieve big things. God wants to do big things in you.

It is not just who you hang around, it is also about what you put into your thought life. Have you ever gone to a movie, started reading a book or watching a TV show and something is said or done that does not align with your beliefs? You have a choice to make. Do you continue to watch or read it? Do you sometimes let things slide by, not wanting to make a big deal about it in front of others? Or do you think that this one little thing will not matter, so you just sit there allowing that influence to go into your thought life? Pictures are the worst. Once you have seen an image that you know is inappropriate, it is difficult to get that image out of your mind. The best defense is to not allow it in the first place. Be careful what you put in your mind because it can slowly take on a life of its own. Before you know it, you cannot determine how you got to where you are. Be intentional in what you watch, read and listen to.

Intentional Growth Is a Choice

When you wake up each day, be deliberate and intentional in your actions and decisions. Ask God for His guidance and leadership that day and align yourself with what He has planned. Live life in such a way that you are open to whatever God has planned for you. Hold onto your plans loosely. When God puts something unexpected, unplanned in front of you, do not disregard it. God places people and situations in your life to help you accomplish your destiny and purpose. Walk each day expecting that God is going to show up and lead you. Any chance you get to work with God is an exciting adventure which you should look forward to. Adjust your plans accordingly when the opportunity presents itself and allow God to do amazing things with and through you.

Focus your energy on positioning yourself to learn all you can about the things that you are feeling called to or those dreams that are deep within you. Read books, go to conferences, shadow someone, join a study group, find a mentor that will walk beside you on your journey. Being intentional in our growth can require some stepping out of our comfort zones as we explore new experiences, new revelations, and new opportunities. Sometimes it requires us to step out financially to get the resources we need to succeed and grow. Everything you put into the growth toward your vision will be worth the risk, the investment, and the time. God will do marvelous things as you step into the vision He has for you.

Prayer for Leaving Chance Behind – Choosing to Be Intentional
By Cinda Gregory

"Heavenly Father, I realize and admit that I have not stewarded my life and my calling as intentionally as I should have…I repent and ask that You would forgive me. I choose this day to change. I choose to embrace this day as a new beginning.

I thank You Father that I have a hope and a future. That I am not on this earth just to wander aimlessly. I have a destiny and a purpose. I have been created to fulfill a calling that only I can fulfill! I want to be the best I can be. Father, I no longer want to live a haphazard life with little or no direction. I want to be like an arrow, shot forth out of Your bow, destined to hit the target and accomplish its purpose. Father, from this day forward I choose to partner with You deliberately and intentionally so I can do this. In areas of my life that need to be pruned and adjusted, I give you permission to do what You know is best for me. I trust You, Father. In areas I need to grow, I ask Father that You would help me to design a very practical growth plan that can become a lifestyle for me. I also ask that You bring leaders around me to encourage me. Bring people into my life that can walk with me and help me to grow.

Father, I ask right now that You would give me a glimpse of how You see me. Give me a glimpse of what You created me for, a glimpse of the hope and the future that You have for me. Your word says that without vision your people perish, so Father I am asking for vision…give me a vision that is bigger than myself. A vision of who I was meant to be and how that will impact the world around me. Thank you, Father.

I choose right now to partner with that vision. I choose to fully embrace my calling and my destiny. Father, I choose right now to engage with You and do what I need to do to make it happen. I choose

Yes! Yes, I will prepare. Yes, I will deliberately and intentionally grow so that I can impact the world for Your Kingdom. Yes, I will do what I can do, God, so You can do what only YOU can do! I rebuke all lethargy and choose this day to fully embrace whatever it is I need to do to become trained and prepared. Thank you, Father, for choosing ME to be a world-changer! Amen." [29]

Parenting Without an Identity Crisis – Choosing to Separate Your Kid's Mistakes from Your Identity

Key #5 – Partnering With God Is a Choice

Day 1:
SURRENDERING YOUR CHILDREN TO JESUS

The shelves in the bookstore are lined with books on how to be a "great" parent. They are full of the ins and outs of parenting and what the experts say parents should and should not do. I have yet to find a book that solved all my parenting issues. There is no perfect teaching on parenting; our only lessons are learned through the fire of parenting.

> "Making the decision to have a child is momentous – it is to decide forever to have your heart go walking around outside your body."[30] (Elizabeth Stone, *Village Voice*)

Parenting is a tough job; perhaps one of the toughest. From the moment you lay your eyes on that newborn baby, your heart is never just yours again. Your world changes, and suddenly you are more vulnerable than you were before because you no longer are dealing with your own heart. You are intertwined with another heart, which you cannot always protect, and you have no control over. When your children are young, you tend to feel that you can protect them from the world. You make choices for them believing you are doing the right thing for them. The problem with that thinking is you cannot be with your child one hundred percent of the time. Once they begin school, start making friends, go to church or camp, the world will creep in. Sometimes even with our best intentions, things do not go the way we planned. We lose our control. Control can be a good thing, but it also can lead to devastating results. Control, or one could say manipulation, has a way of eventually blowing up in our faces.

Many parents are walking around with regrets, guilt, shame, and broken hearts because of their children's lives. As parents, we have had dreams and hopes for our children, only to see many of the dreams shattered. Maybe that is part of the problem. We have dreams, but are our dreams the dreams that God has planted in the heart of our child? Could we sometimes be pushing our child toward what we think they should be, instead of allowing God to speak His dreams to their hearts?

Some of you have seen your children walk through: drug addiction, alcohol addiction, depression, sexual immorality, divorce and many other life choices that have broken your heart and left you with a heap of guilt. You ask yourself, what could I have done better? Some of you have lost a child to death, and the gaping hole within your heart never seems to mend. Others have experienced a sense of profound loss when their children walked completely out of their lives leaving them wondering day after day if they are okay and if they will ever return. The overwhelming sense of guilt, shame, and all the "what if's" can be consuming. Parenting is a blessing, but it also can be one of the most heart-breaking things we experience.

Mary, the mother of Jesus, experienced devastating heartbreak throughout her son's life, from the temple courts when Simeon told Mary that a sword would pierce her heart, to standing at the foot of the cross watching her son die. The pain was unbearable, but she knew that God had planned His life from the moment the angel announced the coming of Jesus to her. Mary humbled herself before the Lord and gave herself to Him to be used as the woman who would bear the Son of God. But even so, this was her child that God gave her to raise. She loved Him from the moment she gave birth to Him, but she knew Jesus was God's child.

Surrendering Your Children to Jesus

I had just put the kids down for their nap and decided to go out to the porch and read a book from my favorite author at the time. I sat down on my chair in the warm sun and started reading the book "Splashes of Joy in the Cesspools of Life" by Barbara Johnson. I was enjoying the book until I got to a chapter that contained a section about giving your children up to the Lord. God was about to unravel my world for the next few hours.

At that time my husband had just attended a Christian retreat, an "Emmaus weekend," in Elizabethtown, Kentucky. The weekend was life changing for him. He could not wait for me to go on the weekend and experience what he had just experienced. He returned home from the weekend and announced, "You are going on the next women's weekend." I was not happy about that. My son was just over a year old and my daughter, three. I was not about to leave my babies for three and a half days. On top of that, he told me that his residency program was going to Atlanta for a dental conference the same four days, so he would arrange for someone from our Church to care for our children. Now I was adamant. "Nope, I was not going!" My husband was persistent and headed back to work unknowingly leaving me in a puddle of tears and frustration.

God was beginning to reveal to me that I was wrestling deep within because I did not trust Him to take care of my family. My husband was not the issue; it was my issue … did I believe that if God called me to go away that He would take care of my children while I was gone? I hated the thought that I did not trust God. My head trusted Him, but my heart was not saying the same thing. I was miserable. I knew what He was calling me to do. The question was, would I surrender my children to Him? I felt the anxiety building and knew that this was a battle that I did not want to fight. I sat staring at the book wondering if I could surrender my children to God. I was so thankful to God for blessing me with my children. But I had forgotten that they were His before the beginning of time.

God kept bringing me back to surrender: "giving them to Him." As I turned the page of the book, crying, a blurry picture came into focus. It was a picture of Jesus sitting on the throne with a child in His arms. Jesus was playfully lifting him up in the air. The child was smiling. In front of the throne was a long flight of stairs. Barbara Johnson encouraged her readers to imagine yourself wrapping your child as a gift and then climbing that long flight of stairs with your child in your arms, keeping your eyes on Jesus as you took each step. When you reach the top of the stairs, carefully hand your (gift) child over to Jesus. Watch as Jesus takes your gift and unwraps it. Visualize as Jesus lifts your child and places your child onto His lap. When I watched Jesus take my son and placed him in His lap and wrapped His arms around him, the love I sensed was overwhelming. I saw Jesus smile at him. The love He had for him was indescribable. The hardest act of all, I had to turn and walk down those stairs, leaving my child in Jesus' arms. Barbara Johnson said, "Be sure to turn around and look occasionally to see that he is safe in the arms of Jesus."[31] I began crying and I knew that it was time to fully entrust my children to Jesus. The fact that I held onto them so tightly spoke volumes on whose children I thought they were. I found myself on my knees sobbing saying, "Jesus, they are yours." Some of you need to walk up that flight of stairs. It is time to give your children to the One who can lead them into the destiny for which He created them.

That moment was life changing. I no longer carried the burden for how my children were going to be throughout life; I had given them to Jesus to do as He saw fit. I have done this for all my children. I can say that at times I have tried to take them back or have acted as if I had taken them back, but quickly I find myself returning them to the One who can be their constant companion, the One who knows their every thought, knows their every action. The One who knows their destiny and purpose, the One who loves them even more than I do. They are safe in the Father's arms, and I need to trust God with them. So do you. This one act has changed my life as a parent. Instead of trying to control and manipulate, I find myself more often on my knees pouring out my heart for my children. The Father

84

hears our heart and our prayers, combining these with His great love for them, He will continue to draw our children as they walk into their future. God does not give up on our children. He never will. Our job as parents is to keep praying for them to respond to God's calling on their lives. Pray that their eyes would be opened to see God and that their hearts would be softened to hear His voice.

How tightly are you holding onto your children? On a scale of 1 to 10 (1 being you are very loose, casual, and 10 being tightly reined in and wielding total control)

1　　2　　3　　4　　5　　6　　7　　8　　9　　10

Why do you think you hold onto your children so tightly or loosely?

Is it time for you to climb those stairs and surrender your children to God? Do you need to ask God for forgiveness for taking your children back and not trusting Him with them?

Bible Parents Who Struggled

King David, the man after God's own heart, showed some very disastrous parenting skills. From his four wives, David had twenty sons (one died at birth) and one daughter (Tamar). Although David loved God, he did not just naturally become a great parent. He had difficulty from the very start. His first child was conceived out of an adulterous relationship, which led to David killing Bathsheba's husband, Uriah. Amnon, David's firstborn (from Jezreel), became filled with lust and raped his half-sister, Tamar. Absalom, David's third son (from Maacah), planned the murder of his half-brother, Amnon in revenge for the rape of his sister Tamar. He then plotted to steal his Father's throne by endearing himself to the people, causing David to flee his city. Absalom then decided that it would be good to have sex with David's concubines in plain view of everyone. Absalom died in battle and then David returned to the throne. (2 Samuel 13-19)

David's family was out of control, and he did nothing to try to correct them. He did not discipline them; instead, he ran away from his troubles. David's fourth son, Adonijah tried to become king and take the throne away from Solomon who was the rightful heir. Solomon had Adonijah executed for trying to steal the throne (1 Kings 2:25). One could say that even though David loved God with all his heart, his parenting skills were less than stellar. Still God loved him and blessed his lineage that eventually led to the Messiah being born.

Solomon was a great King and pleased God. God granted Solomon wisdom and great wealth. Solomon followed God, but there were two errors he made: he married women that worshipped other gods (which God had forbidden him to do), and he failed to remove the high places where his wives' idols were worshiped. This was his downfall.

We think parenting is difficult, but what about Mary and Joseph? I often wonder what it would have been like to be the earthly parents of Jesus. I am sure there were plenty of times they questioned their ability to raise the Son of God. What ran through their minds when they realized they had left Jesus behind in Jerusalem without noticing He was not with them? When they returned a few days later, they found Jesus in the temple preaching. Can you hear their sighs of relief, and the stress in their voice when they asked Jesus what He was doing?

I can relate to this story. My family had gone to the New York State Fair with some of our relatives. It was evening and the sun was beginning to go down and some of our group wanted to go on the giant Ferris wheel and see the lights of the fair. My fear of heights kept me from going so I walked around while they went on the ride. About a half hour later we met up by the Ferris wheel entrance. When I looked at my husband and the rest of the group I asked, "Where is Ben?" My husband responded, "He was with you." And as fear gripped my heart, I responded, "No, he was with you!" The midway was packed with people and my five-year-old son was missing! We quickly divided up and each group took an isle of the midway to search. I immediately began praying like never before, as I was now in a total panic. I kept asking God to protect him and lead us to him. Suddenly, in the middle of the packed midway, there was this opening (or circle) where there was not a person, which was immediately obvious and noticeable. There, standing in the center of the opening, was my son. Emotions flooded me. I was so upset that I did not know what to do. I ran to my son and embraced him with the tightest hug with which I think I have ever hugged someone. As I held him in my arms, I kept thanking the Lord for leading us to Ben and that he was okay. I am sure Mary and Joseph felt the same sense of relief when they found Jesus in the temple.

What was it like for Mary and Joseph to raise the "Son of God" amongst their other children? We do not know when Joseph died, but Mary was thrust into the role of a single parent to the Son of God! How did she handle Jesus' siblings when they teased Jesus and did not believe that He was the Son of God? What did Mary feel when she saw Jesus performing miracle after miracle? Was her heart bursting with pride and joy? How did she persevere when she saw Jesus being abused, whipped and crucified? Her role as parent was heart wrenching. No, parenting is not easy, regardless of who you are.

Identity Displaces Fear

When we hold onto our children too tightly, we are generally operating out of "fear". We try to protect our children from the pain, sickness, trauma and cruelty of the world. We may have experienced something in our childhood or teen years that we never want our children to experience, so we try

hard to steer them away from certain things in hopes that we can protect them. Fear can lead us to holding our children so tightly that they are never allowed to explore the person God intended them to be. We all need to discover who we are. When we learn our identity through God's eyes, we no longer need to be fearful. Do not listen to the enemy saying who he thinks you are because all he speaks is lies. God sees you as a conqueror, victorious and strong. You are "chosen by God," "you are God's beloved," the "light of the world," the "salt of the earth." God wants us to speak this to our children. However, perhaps some of you first need to speak it to yourself.

God's view of who they are is the most essential voice they need to hear. Who we are and who we are meant to be should never be dictated by someone else or society. If you are allowing others to dictate your identity you are going to live in a state of confusion, never measuring up. Our success as people cannot be integrated in the behavior of our children, spouse, parents, or our career. When we do this, we are setting ourselves up for a life of unhappiness. We need to take care not to over-identify with our children and thus begin to live vicariously through them.

Cinda wrote in her book:

> "Allowing my self-worth and self-image to be directly tied to parenting created a recipe for disaster. I was caught on a hamster wheel so oblivious I had no idea that I needed to get off. If the girls were doing great, it meant I was a good mom. If they were perfect, it meant I was perfect. If they were well-liked and accepted, I was accepted as well. On and on it went. However, it actually went much deeper than that. It did not mean that I was just accepted as a mom, doing great as a mom, or was perfect as a mom. It meant that as a PERSON I was accepted, great, and perfect. My entire identity was yoked to parenting. If they looked good to the world, I was a good person. But as soon as they publicly misbehaved in any way, as children do, I came undone. I felt worthless, rejected, lacking, insignificant, and a thousand other emotions that would speak death to my fragile ego."[32]

Parents can live vicariously through their children. When their child succeeds, they feel like they succeed, but when their children fail or choose a path you do not agree with, you feel like a failure and your self-esteem plummets. Parents who suffer from low self-esteem are more likely to fall into this "trap of the enemy."

Have I sought my identity through my children instead of what God thinks of me?

Cinda talks about an "unspoken code" that made her children responsible for determining whether she was a valuable person.

"…it was apparent that there was a critical part missing: the healthy, unconditional love that we had seen openly displayed in other families was absent in ours. Unfortunately, because of our insecurities, Bob and I had modeled an extremely conditional love to our girls."[33]

Conditional love never works because it is not love; it is control. We cannot control anyone else. Therefore, putting our identity in the hands of our children is a dangerous thing. We were never meant to get our identity from our children, but from God.

Do I love unconditionally? Ask the Lord to help you love like Him.

Day 2:
DO YOUR KIDS A FAVOR – DROP YOUR BAGGAGE

Shortly after I moved to New York, I walked through a time in my life where my self-esteem hit rock bottom. I had moments where all I wanted to do was escape, move, or even just go be in heaven where things were not so painful. At nighttime I would beg God to take me as I laid on my bed, but I kept hearing God say, "There is hope in Me." He did not say there was hope for me because of my children (although they were the reason I wanted to live). No, there was hope because He is a God of hope. My issue was I did not know who I was. I did not know deep within me the value I had because of who I was, a child of God. I made it through that rough time by pouring out my heart to God, lying on the ground and just soaking in the words of worship music. I had no attention span to sit and read the Bible for more than a few minutes, but the words of the worship music began to breathe life back into my soul. But there was fallout, and I became very controlling and manipulative toward my children and others because I could not take the risk of having my world fall apart again.

It was my issue, not my children's. It started as a young child when I was molested by my next-door neighbor. From that point on I never talked about what happened. I had an amazing mother, but she always talked about "sexual" things negatively. How could I ever tell her what happened? She would be disgusted with me and so disappointed. Shame was already taking hold of me. It was easier to keep quiet and never mention it. I remember going with mom in 5th grade to my Elementary School to see "the movie." Back in the late 60's, and early 70's, sex education was taught by showing a movie which your parents brought you to under the darkness of night! I remember driving home with silence in the car. There was never any other discussion about it. Not how wonderful sex could be…nothing. Silence spoke to my shame. As I matured, I wanted to be loved so badly. I had several boyfriends, but I always ended up with a broken heart which taught me once again I was not worthy

of being loved and people could not be trusted. I began to believe that something was wrong with me; I was not a good person.

I remember one time when my family went skiing up north and my fiancé came with us. After eating lunch, I had decided to not go back out on the slopes due to an injury on my leg. As my fiancé got up to leave with my family, I wrapped my arm around his leg and patted his knee. When everyone had left the table, my mother scolded me and told me how inappropriate I was and that the "whole ski lodge was watching me." Shame descended upon me again.

I married my high school sweetheart in 1981, who quickly learned of the baggage I carried into marriage. It was buried so deep within me, like the roots of a tree, that I never realized how deeply affected I had been. I pretty much had blocked it out of my memory until it surfaced once again when a young man I worked with was arrested for molestation of a young child in the preschool class I was teaching. It was during his trial that my childhood memories came back, and it almost destroyed me. My husband was so worried about me, and quite frankly, did not know how to help me. It was during this time I wished I could just die to escape the emotional pain I was going through. A lot of people hated me because I had no evidence to testify against this young man. I never saw anything that sent up red flags, and people did not believe me. There was even an editorial in the local paper deriding me. I literally was afraid to go out on the street, fearing that someone would run me over if they had a chance. My self-hatred escalated at this time and depression set in.

We ended up leaving our church because of reasons related to the trial, so we were without a church from May till mid-November. This broke my heart because I loved so many people at my church. It was at this time that I literally begged God to find a church for us. I knew that God was my source of hope and my restoration could only be found in Him. God led us to a little church in the country. The moment we walked in we knew we were home. Not a song had been sung or a sermon preached; it was just the presence of God when we walked in – we could feel it. For the first couple of months when the worship music began, my tears began to flow. God continued to use worship to heal my broken heart.

In January, a guest pastor came to the church. He was known for being a prophet. I was not sure what I believed about "prophets", but I felt like we were supposed to go. The prophet began speaking and then all of a sudden turned and looked at my husband and I and began speaking to us about everything we had just walked through, as well as other things from the past that were personal to us. I jokingly whispered to my husband "He was reading our mail and that he was directly downloading from God." After speaking many things that only God could have told him, he began to prophesy that God was mending our broken hearts and then he spoke of the future. That was a turnaround point, from that time on God did a tremendous healing in us. God never intended us to remain in a place of brokenness. He wanted us free.

So why did I share all this? All this impacted me as a parent. The filter I was using as a parent was not clean, it was covered with lots of dirt from my past. This led me to try to protect my children desperately, keeping them on a tight leash. I know they called me "momma bear" and quite often I was. To this day I am still a momma bear, but not just for my kids but for any child I see that is the underdog, the one being bullied, the one being left out. Children, and people in general, need cheerleaders today more than ever. Your value has no bearing on anyone else. Your value is from God who chose you, created you and loves you. You are valuable because you are His. The job of others is to walk alongside you, to encourage you and cheer you on in your journey. We are called to be cheerleaders for our children. When they fail, we cheer them on to not give up, to try again, to believe in themselves.

Do I have any dirt on my lens from the past that effects the clarity of what I am seeing?

What baggage do I need to drop? What memories, feelings, emotions, offensives from the past have I held onto that I need to let go of?

Ask the Lord to meet you in this place, to reveal the truth of past situations to you. Ask forgiveness where forgiveness is needed. Surrender those things that you have held onto so tightly to Jesus. Pour out your heart to Jesus and allow Him to heal you from your brokenness.

Day 3:
LOVE IS THE FOUNDATION

Cinda stated that "rules without relationship led to rebellion."[34] Rules and discipline are important for children, but if we are constantly pounding rules upon our children and not infusing unconditional love into them, they will often rebel. Discipline when properly applied to our children builds up love and trust, encourages respect for others, and teaches children about the nature of God. It is our job to train, mold, correct, guide, punish, reward, instruct, warn, teach, and love our kids.

"For their command is a lamp and their instruction a light; their corrective discipline is the way to life." Proverbs 6:23 (NLT)

"For this command is a lamp, this teaching is a light, and correction and instruction are the way to life." Proverbs 6:23 (NIV)

"Good friend, follow your father's good advice; don't wander off from your mother's teachings. Wrap yourself in them from head to foot; wear them like a scarf around your neck. Wherever you walk, they'll guide you; whenever you rest, they'll guard you; when you wake up, they'll tell you what's next. For sound advice is a beacon, good teaching is a light, moral discipline is a life path." Proverbs 6:23 (MSG)

"For the commandment is a lamp; and the law is light; and reproofs of instruction are the way of life." Proverbs 6:23 (KJV)

When parents balance love when giving correction, children will flourish. Children notice the things you love, what you sacrifice for and where your priorities are. They see where you spend your time and with whom. Much of what they are learning about love is what they are observing in you. What kind of love are your children viewing? God laid the foundation of sacrificial love and what it looks like. Sacrificial love speaks value, respect, gratitude, grace, and forgiveness.

These attributes model love. Children and adults are much more likely to comply to rules when they know they are loved. It is the love that changes our response. It is never too late to begin to model sacrificial love to your children, regardless of their age.

The Pharisees were great rule makers. The harshness they placed on people to follow the Scriptures and their man-made rules caused people to be burdened and exasperated. The Pharisees were controlling and manipulating, displaying extraordinarily little love. As a result, Jesus spent a lot of His ministry trying to correct the Pharisees attitudes and clean up their messes.

The message Jesus gave was that God loves each person, even if they were head deep in sin. He never stopped reaching out to them, speaking life and hope to them and showing them a better way. Jesus constantly spoke about how all our actions should be motivated by our love for God. We are called to have that kind of love for our children and to the people that God puts in our life. We are to have unconditional love. Love was never meant to be conditional. Our love should look for the best in our children and others, not to be standing just waiting for them to make a mistake. God demonstrates over and over what love looks like. His love is given all the time, regardless of what we do or do not do.

What does Matthew 7:12 say about love?

What kind of love do I display to my children?

What changes do I need to make in my life for unconditional love to flow out of me?

Misfit to Beloved

When I was 44, God answered the cry of my heart and gave me a third child. I had two beautiful children, but I always wanted to have more. My first pregnancy was greatly anticipated after eight years of marriage. My husband was so thrilled that we were going to have a child that he would go to the German market and buy flowers for me. At one time I felt like I was living in a flower shop rather than a small German apartment. The flowers stopped coming when I unexpectedly had a miscarriage that eventually landed me in the hospital with a severe infection and concern of me becoming sterile. God in His goodness allowed me to get pregnant again two months later and I had a beautiful daughter. Two years later, I was blessed with a son. I always wanted more children, but it was not until seven years later that I got pregnant again and then miscarried. The miscarriage affected my son so severely that I decided to stop trying to have any more children. God had a plan that I was unaware of at the time. Thirteen years after Ben was born, God blessed me with another son at 44 years old. His timing was not my timing, but it was God's perfect plan.

It was shortly after my son, Samuel, was born that I literally went through an identity crisis. The friends I had for years that I had raised my other two kids with were sending their children off to college and having lots of time to do things they wanted to do. I was used to going out to lunch, shopping, and visiting with friends whenever I wanted. But now I was home during the day following the demanding schedule of a baby. I found myself being home alone, and my social life was disappearing quickly. I took my son to story hour one day with my youth pastors' wife (who was in her twenties). While we were there, the young moms were planning a play date and invited Meagan right away. Then as almost an afterthought, they said, "You can come with your grandson if you want." I realized then that I had become a misfit. I no longer fit with my friends I had for years, and now I did not really fit with the young moms.

It was during this time that God began to show me my identity and that it had nothing to do with my stage in life. I belonged to Him. No matter who was or was not in my life, my identity was

completely settled in what God thought of me. He chose this time for me to be a mom, and I began to embrace my new role as a mother of two teenagers and now a baby. The time of feeling like a "misfit" vanished as I embraced my time at home alone with my baby. God had heard the cry of my heart years before. Yet even before my heart cried out, He had planned for Samuel. God showed me during these "lonely" days that I am never alone, that His love for me was so great that I will never comprehend it. He taught me that miracles happen in His time. As the years have flown by and my other two children are married and living their lives, my youngest is still home with me. I am treasuring these moments and praise God for His perfect timing.

What areas in my life has my identity been intertwined with the opinions and actions of others?

Where have I allowed others (my children) to determine my value? Where have I allowed the actions and words of others to determine my worth?

Memorial Stones – God's Faithfulness

It is important to talk about the faithfulness of God with your children. Make it a habit to share with your children how God has been faithful in your life and in theirs!

What do the following Scriptures encourage parents to do?

Isaiah 38:19

Deuteronomy 6:6-9

It is easy for children and adults to not see where God has moved in their behalf. As parents, it is critical that we point it out to them. When we make a habit of speaking about God's faithfulness and how His word directs our path, our children will begin to see the importance of it in their own lives as they grow and mature.

Please read Joshua 3:14-4:24 – the story of the Israelites crossing the Jordan River.

What happened when the priests who carried the ark reached the Jordan and their feet touched the water?

What did the Israelites do?

What did the stones symbolize?

What does Joshua 4:21 state?

Why did God do this?

The memorial stones were to be used by the Israelites to teach their children about God. As parents we need to have traditions – special days, special places to help our children learn about God's work in their life.

One tradition my husband and I established from the moment we had children was on Christmas day to have a birthday cake for Jesus, complete with candles. We gather around after dinner and light the candles and sing Happy Birthday to Jesus. Our children from the very beginning knew that Christmas was a celebration of Jesus' birth. Having the cake is the perfect reminder at the end of an often-busy Christmas day. Jesus, the perfect gift, has come to earth!

Encourage your children to write down those times when God did something special in their life: when He gave them to you, answered their prayers, healed them, supplied for their needs or how God just displayed who He was to them. These "markers" are important to write down because they remind them of God's faithfulness. Make it a habit to share how faithful God has been in your life and what He is doing currently in your life. God wants to be a part of your daily life. Children need to know that God is not just God of the "Sundays", but He is the God of Monday, Tuesday, Wednesday, Thursday, Friday, and Saturday!!! He is here now with you, and He is preparing the future for them.

What are some memorial stones from your life?

What memorial stones have you seen in your children's lives?

Day 4:
TIME TO OWN IT

We have all fallen short of the mark of "perfect parents." We will make lousy choices at one time or another, and unfortunately when we make bad choices it will affect others. Being less than perfect does not make any of us less valuable, it just shows that we are human, living in this imperfect world.

What does James 1:5 state?

God gives us wisdom to recognize not only our mistakes but to correct them. God wants us to live the abundant life, which includes having God's wisdom. I have learned that some of the greatest wisdom God gives me is learning to "surrender" those people or things that consume my mind with worry and concern. Admitting I have made mistakes, I allow God to take my mess and make something beautiful out of it. God takes our lives and makes "beauty from ashes." He can turn all things around.

My Ways Are Not Your Ways

God welcomes our questions. But it is up to the Lord what He wants to reveal to us or explain to us. If He chooses not to explain to us, it is His sovereign knowledge, and therefore we do not have to know or understand His thinking. While it is okay to ask God questions, we are to never challenge God on His sovereignty. God can do what He wants to do and what He knows is best. We are not to question His decisions; our role is to accept it.

Complete the following Scriptures about God's ability to direct our lives?

Isaiah 48:17

"I am the Lord your God, who _____ you what is _____ for you, who _____ you in the way you should go." (NIV)

Proverbs 3:5-6

Trust in the Lord with _____ your heart and lean _____ on your _____ understanding; in _____ your ways _____ to him, and he will make your paths straight." (NIV)

Isaiah 55:8-9

"For my thoughts are _____ your thoughts, neither are _____ ways my ways," declares the Lord. "As the heavens are higher than the earth, so are my _____ higher than your ways and _____ thoughts than your thoughts." (NIV)

When we embrace the fact that we do not have to understand everything, we will be walking in faith. I think of the saying "on a need-to-know basis." If we have the need to know, He will let us know. Otherwise, we walk by faith knowing that the God who created all things, the God that is eternal and the God that is all knowing, has us covered.

> *"Do you not know? Have you not heard? The Lord is the everlasting God, the Creator of the ends of the earth, He will not grow tired or weary, and his understanding no one can fathom. He gives strength to the weary and increases the power of the weak. Even youths grow tired and weary and young men stumble and fall; but those who hope in the Lord will renew their strength. They will soar on wings like eagles; they will run and not grow weary; they will walk and not be faint." Isaiah 40:28-31 (NIV)*

Our job is to let go of our struggles, worries and concerns and believe that God knows what He is doing. And while we wait on Him, He will increase our power and strengthen us. Our job is to trust, let go and believe.

Day 5:
YOU ARE YOUR CHILDREN'S WATCHMAN

> *"Be watchful, stand firm in the faith, act like men, be strong. Let all that you do be done in love." 1 Corinthians 16:13-14 (ESV)*

> *"Be on your guard; stand firm in the faith; be courageous; be strong. Do everything in love." 1 Corinthians 16:13-14 (NIV)*

Although these Scripture were not written about parenting, it is a good framework for parenthood as well as a good principle to instill in our children. Studying God's Word is the closest thing we have to the perfect parenting manual. For when we study God's Word, and let it transform our heart and mind, our actions toward our children begin to look different. When we apply what we learn to the way we parent, God is in the driver's seat.

Being Watchful

There are many Scriptures in the Bible that refer to watchmen. In ancient times, you would find the watchman stationed in a tower in the large walls that surrounded a city. These walls were for much needed protection, and it was the watchman's job to keep an eye on any potential dangers. If the watchman saw an enemy approaching, he would sound the alarm by blowing into a horn. The watchman was expected to stay awake and alert and watch the horizon with careful attention for any dangers. The watchman had to be faithful, not fearful, and aware that the safety of many people was his responsibility.

God chose you to be the watchman for your children. It is your job to watch and listen for any potential dangers, and when you see one, it is your job to sound the alarm. Protect, defend, and instruct your child in what is needed to be done to keep him or her safe. No matter what the age of your child, a parent never stops being their watchman.

What characteristics does a watchman have according to Proverbs 8:32-35?

An important characteristic of the watchman is that they are patient and can wait. When we are watching we are also listening and waiting. As a parent it is easy to become distracted and lose our focus on what is important. It is your job as a parent to: wait patiently, listen, watch, and meditate on God's Word for direction.

I was always intrigued with the Scripture that described Joshua standing outside of the tent of meeting while Moses went in to meet with God.

> *"Whenever the people saw the pillar of cloud standing at the entrance to the tent, they all stood and worshiped, each at the entrance to his tent. The Lord would speak to Moses face to face, as a man speaks with his friend. Then Moses would return to the camp, but his young aide Joshua son of Nun did not leave the tent." Exodus 33:10-11 (NIV)*

When Moses' came out of the tent, Joshua was there to see Moses' reaction of his meeting with God. What happened next was interesting, after Moses left, Joshua did not leave. He lingered near the tent, the place where God's presence was. Lingering in God's presence makes the difference in our parenting. Pray about the situations your children are experiencing and then wait to hear from the Lord. When we wait and linger on the Lord, our interactions with our children will often be different.

Standing Firm in Our Place

The older your kids get the more difficult parenting becomes. Your children mature and start making their own decisions, and your desires may or may not matter all the time. This is when it is critical to stand firm and not lose hope. Some of you are looking at your situation with your child/children as hopeless. With God there is no such word as "hopeless." When things seem out of control, falling on our knees and delving into the Scriptures is the only place we can go. Trust in the Lord and believe that He will respond to your prayers. God hears every cry of our heart, and He acts on those prayers. Stand in confidence that God is going to direct you as a parent onto the right path that will help change the situation you are dealing with.

What do the following Scriptures say about standing firm?

1 Corinthians 16:13

2 Corinthians 1:24

Colossians 1:23

It may take time…stand firm in God's promises.

> "*Train up a child in the way he should go, and when he his old he will not depart from it.*"
> *Proverbs 22:6 (NKJV)*

Some of you may be thinking, "But I did not raise up my child in the Lord." Our God is big, your prayers are heard: "The effectual fervent prayer of a righteous man availeth much." (James 5:16, KJV) It is never too late. God wants nothing more than to draw your adult children unto him. Stand Firm. Believe.

> "*When he entered the house, the blind men came to him, and Jesus said to them, "Do you believe that I am able to do this?" They said to him, "Yes, Lord." Then he touched their eyes, saying, "According to your faith be it done to you."*" *Matthew 9:28-29 (ESV)*

In the Scripture above what question did Jesus ask Blind Bartimaeus?

After touching His eyes what did Jesus say?

Be Strong and Courageous
What do the Scriptures below tell us to do? What do they say God will do?

Joshua 1:9

2 Chronicles 32:7-8

Although both these Scriptures were spoken to the Israelites as they were preparing for battle, they are true for us today. We as parents, and our children, will encounter many battles throughout our journey in life. But God calls us to be strong and courageous as we face all that the enemy, or our own choices, throw in our direction. We can be confident that the Lord God is here to help us fight our battles and direct our path if we give our lives to Him.

Looking back at my parenting, I can see where my desire to be my children's "friend" instead of being the "parent" got me into trouble. A friend once described me as a marshmallow. She is right. My family teases me because I watch way too much Hallmark Channel, especially at Christmas time. I want to live in a "fairytale world" where everything turns out in the end, and we all live happily ever after. So, raising kids has been challenging for me. It often is not the fairy tale and more like the "Survivor". As your kids grow, they develop their own opinions and start making decisions for themselves without consulting mom or dad. There are times when they say things that upset you or talk back to you in disrespect. There are times they openly are defiant and do not listen to you or obey you.

There are different ways of handling our emotions of anger, frustration, and disappointment. It is in these times that we must choose to take the high road. When we engage out of our emotions, irreparable damage can happen that takes years to heal. I have experienced this firsthand. Sometimes what is required of us is walking away from the situation. Being strong and courageous enough to not engage in the destructive power of the tongue. Closing our mouth and seeking God's direction for how to respond to a situation is exhibiting strong character. Mike and Marilyn Phillipps of Marriage Ministries International (MMI), called it a "strife break." When our emotions are running high, it is never a good time to try to solve differences. It is time for an adult time out. It takes courage and strength in the Lord to step back. It is important to be confident in the Lord's power to lead you as a parent.

> *"Fathers, do not provoke your children to anger, but bring them up in the discipline and instruction of the Lord." Ephesians 6:4 (ESV)*

I must admit I made a lot of mistakes in this area. I learned that you cannot operate out of what you think or feel. My son and I are complete opposites. From the minute he would speak I felt like he was always challenging me and that we were never on the same page. It seemed like we argued about everything. We argued about homework, we argued about how much time he spent on the computer, and we even argued about why he did not go out with his friends when they invited him to do something. When we argued, there was never yelling involved because my mode of arguing was lecturing. I would get on a point and repeat it over and over until I thought it had finally gotten into his head. Now I look back and realize that after the first time of expressing my feelings the conversation was over, nothing was being processed that I was saying, and I had become obnoxious in the eyes of my child. I had no idea how to handle confrontations. So, if I did not want to get on the arguing and lecturing soapbox, I would just retreat and ignore the situation. Sometimes it was easier to retreat and not engage because I felt like less of a failure as a parent. When I did engage, I often walked away with my feelings hurt by something that was said. I was good at provoking my son to anger, although never intentionally. All my dreams of being my son's friend were totally gone, and now I just wanted to somehow survive being his parent. I never felt more like a failure than I did in my relationship with my son. The very thing I yearned so badly for, a close relationship, was the one thing I never seemed able to get. There was no doubt that we loved each other; we just had no idea how to communicate.

I remember when my son was nineteen and went off to college. I was praying for him one day and while I was praying, God gave me a revelation about my son. He said, "You know Ben is an introvert?" I was shocked! That explained everything to me. Ben was a talker, especially when it was about something he loved! He would go on and on about his passion. Because of his tendency to sometimes talk non-stop, I felt like he was outgoing, that he was an extrovert. How could I have been so totally wrong for 19 years? It explained so many things; why he did not want to go out with friends and preferred to stay home to finish writing or drawing something. It explained why he did not engage in youth group. Conversations about the deep things were not important at all, and those were the type of conversations that I thrived on. How could I have not understood the very

basics of how God designed my son? I spent so much of my life trying to make him like me, when clearly God had created him into his own unique being. The poor kid was never embraced just for who he was. God never intended Ben to be like me; it was my job to encourage him to be all God intended him to be.

When I look back over my three children's lives, it was Ben's life that I see God was so closely directing. Ben loves history. All his life he has been studying history, drawing history, writing his own stories using historical background. Ben also loves the ocean. One of the first drawings that Ben drew as a toddler was a stick figure of a person with a scuba tank on his back. He lived and dreamed history, ocean, shipwrecks, and scuba diving. Almost every picture he drew in his younger elementary years had a scuba diver in it exploring the ocean. From a young age we knew that Ben was going to do something with history and the ocean. His favorite book was <u>The Discovery of the Titanic</u> by Dr. Robert Ballard, and he attended a lecture at our local university given by Dr. Ballard when he was 9 years old. Of course, he brought his favorite book along to be signed by the author. When he was in high school, Ben began researching colleges that had archaeology programs. For years we had talked about how he would love to study nautical archeology. We even talked about Texas A&M being the best nautical archaeology school in the nation, if not the world. He wanted to go to a Christian college, and it literally seemed impossible to find one that had what he was interested in. So, on a Thursday I called my husband and son to the great room and said, "Let's pray as a family about this situation and ask that God would open the doors." We prayed. God moved. That Sunday we had a guest speaker at church, Dr. Scott Carroll, an archeologist from Cornerstone University in Grand Rapids, Michigan. He brought along with him many Biblical artifacts and shared some amazing Christian historical findings. After church, Ben went up front and began talking to him and before we knew it, Dr. Carroll invited Ben to come visit the college he worked at in Michigan. It just happened that we were heading to Midland, Michigan for the holidays in a few weeks and we agreed to meet him at Cornerstone University in Grand Rapids. Was this a coincidence? I think not.

We toured the abandoned campus during a blizzard. The following Fall, Ben was walking around that campus as an Ancient Studies major learning under Dr. Carrol. During his time at Cornerstone, God was also orchestrating his next step back here in New York by connecting Ben with a professor at Colgate University. Ben had known this man when he was younger and was a friend of his son. This gentleman connected with my husband during a dental appointment, and my husband told him all about Ben and what he was doing. He asked for Ben to come visit him when he came home from school. Before we knew it, he was helping Ben connect with the classics department at the University of Michigan that ran a field project in Rome, Italy. Ben ended up going four consecutive summers to work on an archaeology project just outside of Rome. The professor was now Ben's mentor. Was this a coincidence? I think not.

When it was time to think about graduate school, the professor was critical in helping Ben choose where to apply. Ben is very smart. He has a photographic memory, but he had one big obstacle in his way: the graduate entrance exams required for the master's program. Despite his test anxiety, Ben did well on all parts of the exam. His mentor suggested that Ben apply to Southwestern Theological Seminary where he had recommended him to some of his archaeology colleagues. Ben applied and was accepted. Was this a coincidence? I think not.

The story does not end here. When Ben was finishing up his master's program, he wanted to go on for his PhD in nautical archaeology. Not confident he could get in because the slots for these programs were so limited, he applied to four schools and to Texas A&M (TAMU), where they have the nautical archeology program. He was accepted into Texas A & M's doctoral program. The chairperson at Southwestern was close to one professor within the department at TAMU, who had highly recommended Ben to his colleague. The candidate board listened! Was this a coincidence? I think not.

Looking back, it is so easy to see where God has directed Ben's life. It has been an amazing journey to watch as Ben just completed his doctoral studies and graduated from Texas A & M with his PhD. He is currently working at Texas A & M as he awaits the more permanent job God has for him. I have confidence God already has the next step planned. He is just waiting for the perfect time to reveal it. God is in control. Our job is to pray our children through the journey, encourage them on and to love them every step of the way.

It is easy to look back at our job of parenting and become very critical of ourselves. We all have stumbled our way through, but your children have something that will make all the difference in their future – a praying parent. Do not underestimate the power of your prayers. Do not give up praying just because you have not seen anything happen yet. Press on, keep praying, keep loving and remember your child was God's first. He loves them and hears your cries in their behalf. You have placed them in good hands. Allow God's plans to unfold in his timing as you partner with Him in prayer for your children.

Let All That You Do Be Done in Love

You have heard the saying that "love conquers all." It is not just a cliché. It is truth. Every single decision and every action you take as a parent should be done through the filter of love. When our eyes are filtered with the love of the Father, we will become the best parents we can be.

Please read the story of the Prodigal Son in Luke 15:11-32.

This story is one of the best examples of what a parent's love for their children should look like. The Father in the story is the heart that God has for us and the heart we should have toward our children. In this story the father displayed many of the keys to good parenting. First, when his son confronted him with his demands for his share of the inheritance, the father allowed his son to make his own decision and leave, trusting that he would come to his senses and return. His son had the freedom to choose, even though his choice was not the father's desire. Secondly, while the son was gone, the father kept believing and trusting that his son would return. Luke 15:20 tells us, "While he was still a long way off, his father saw him." The Father never gave up. Every day he stood at the doorway looking down the road for his son, waiting expectantly. Thirdly, when the father saw the son on the horizon down the road, he instantly forgave him before the son could even speak the words he rehearsed in his mind. Lastly, the father rejoiced and celebrated that his son had returned. He did not punish him, yell at or lecture him. He rejoiced and celebrated. The son experienced the unconditional love of the Father. It is our job to show the love of our Father to our children. No matter what they do, good or bad decisions they make, love your kids.

> *"Love is patient, love is kind. It does not envy, it does not boast, it is not proud. It is not rude, it is not self-seeking, it is not easily angered, it keeps no record of wrongs. Love does not delight in evil but rejoices with the truth. It always protects, always trusts, always hopes, always perseveres. Love never fails." 1 Corinthians 13:4-8 (NIV)*

Paul, in 1 Corinthians 13:1, spoke of love being the "most excellent way." These four verses encompass what it means to love completely. We have heard the list before and many people have it memorized but living it out daily is difficult. It requires total surrender of our own thoughts, emotions and life. It also develops with maturity as we walk our faith out. It is this kind of love that breaks the yoke and sets parents and children free. God's love in us unlocks the prison doors.

Prayer for Choosing to Parent Without an Identity Crisis
by Cinda Gregory

"Heavenly Father, I admit that it is so easy to have my identity entwined with the behavior of my children and those in relationship with me. Sometimes it is so gradual and so deceptive that I do not even see it for what it is. I quiet myself before You, Father, and ask You to identify any areas in my identity that are intertwined with the opinions and actions of others. I ask God that You would come now, as

the Great Physician, and begin a surgery to separate any ties that are not of you. I choose to trust You to do this work.

Sometimes, Father, it gets so muddled that I don't even know who I am without others speaking and defining value or identity to me…I realize now that depending on others to speak value to my identity can be a slippery slope that I do not want to be on. Papa, it is your voice that I want to hear. It is what YOU say about me that matters most! So, Papa, I quiet myself before You and position myself to hear Your voice…what would You like to speak to my heart? Who am I? What was I created for? What do You say about me? Who do You say I am? (Allow God to speak to your heart and write down everything that comes to your mind)

Thank you, Father, for Your words of life! Thank you for Your love for me. Thank You that I am significant! That I matter to You. Not for what I can do, but because of who I am! You love me…Thank you! Father, I ask that You put deep in my heart the truth that You just shared with me. That You would put it so deep in my heart that no man and no circumstance would ever be able to shake it loose. Regardless of what may happen around me, Your truth will always be my mooring, my anchor.

Papa, I admit that in the past I allowed the actions of others to speak to my identity. I allowed the actions and words of others to determine my worth. I repent for allowing anyone other than You to determine my value. By the power vested in me through Jesus Christ, I now break all association and all power that false identities have held over my life. I now recognize them for what they truly are: a trap and a lie. I choose instead to believe only what You speak to me, Father. I choose to only believe the truth. By the power vested in me, I also choose to break off the people-pleasing spirit and the fear of man. Father, the only one I want to fear is You. I want to love what You love and hate what You hate. Let my life be a pleasing, Living Epistle for You. For this I give You thanks. Amen." [35]

Week 6:
Perseverance – Choosing Not to Give Up

Key #6 – Progression Toward Your Vision Is a Choice

Day 1:
FEAR DESTROYS THE WILL TO PERSEVERE

"Many of life's failures are people who did not realize how close they were to success when they gave up." [36] Thomas Edison

Standing at the starting line of the Fourth of July race in a small Upstate New York village, I wondered, *how did I get here and why did I think I could do this?* It all started years before when I used to joke that, "If Satan was to put me in hell, he would make me run." I hated running. I would run a half a block, be totally winded and give up. I never really gave it a chance. I just said, *I can't do this.* Not a good attitude for an employee of a Wellness Center whose job it was to help others exercise to strengthen their bodies. Day after day I would encourage people to press on, do not give up, keep getting stronger, while deep within I had given up before I even got started. I heard some people talking about a race in a nearby town, and my first thought was *I would never do that,* but deep within something gnawed at me. After years of making excuses for myself I decided that I at least needed to try running, before saying I cannot do this. Of course, I could not do it with that thought process. I knew it would be a lot of work, and I was just too lazy to want to do what it required of me. It was time to change my attitude and really see what I could do.

I started training on the tread mill with the director of the Wellness Center guiding me. I began with just running a minute, then walking for two minutes. Gradually I kept making the running intervals longer and the resting intervals shorter. There were times my heart was racing so fast it scared me and I would ask him, "Are you sure I should be doing this?" His response was, "I know what kind of shape you are in and how hard I should push your body. But, if you feel you need to slow down go ahead, but you can do this." As the weeks passed, I began to see that my endurance was gradually being built up and after a few months I was running 45 minutes at a time without taking a break. I never entertained the thought of doing a run in the past, but I could not shake the thought – *I should do this.* I decided to train a little more seriously, and before I knew it, I was registered for the run. I was a nervous wreck. *What if I could not finish, what if I needed to go to the bathroom,* what if … what if … what if?

My daughter and son drove me over the hilly countryside to where the run would begin at 8:00 am. As we parked our car, I saw everyone standing around with their numbers on, some dressed in great running attire, looking excited and ready to go. I walked up to the registration table and was handed my number and slipped it on. It was official, I was going to do my first race. As I lined up among the pack of other runners, I saw my daughter and son watching from a distance. I was proud of myself, and I knew they were proud of me. While other people were cheerfully waiting at the start I just wanted to go to the bathroom and throw up. The gun went off and the pack moved out. It was not long before the "real" runners were far ahead of me. Before I knew it, I was running alone, sometimes with no other runners in sight. I began wondering why I was doing this. I had no idea how far I had run, and I kept thinking the end certainly was near. There were a few moments when I thought I had lost the course and was not sure where I was, but somehow, I ended up on the right road again (sounds like life). I kept telling myself, *I can do this!* And the voice inside said, *Keep running, keep running.*

I ran most of the way, with only a brief walk to catch my breath. About halfway through the run I was thinking the finish line should be just around the corner, but it was not. I pressed on. Time dragged, it seemed like eternity until I began to see the village in the distance, and finally, I could see the finish line. My heart raced with excitement at the thought of the race being almost done. I crossed the finish line and the timer marked my time. My daughter and son were there cheering me on. My son, who was five at the time, said, "Where were you? We have been waiting. You didn't win." I laughed and thought, *at 50 years old my goal was just to run and finish the race.* I did not win the prize, but I felt like it. I had persevered, I had done something that I did not think I could do, and I finished well. I was proud of myself. I had proved to myself that I had more in me than I thought. All the "I cannot do" moments faded away into the thought *"I did it."*

What about you? What race are you running in your life? Some of you are battling cancer, sickness, or disabilities. Some are devastated by broken relationships, children going in the wrong direction, loved ones battling drug, alcohol, sexual additions, death of a loved one, loss of a job or other devastating circumstances. Some of you are just tired. It is not just a race; it is the battle within that is ripping you apart. You are not alone, and God is willing to help you. Do not give up, do not quit.

Keep your eyes on Jesus and press into God and let Him fight your battle for you. He will give you the strength to persevere, the strength to press on. He has good things ahead for you, so hold onto hope. You can do this!!

Merriam-Webster's Dictionary defines perseverance as:

> "To persist in a state, enterprise, or understanding in spite of counter influences, opposition, or discouragement." Synonyms include steadfastness, persistence, tenacity, determination, resolve, resolution and staying power.[37]

Perseverance is patient endurance of hardship, despite difficulties and discouragement. Perseverance is something we learn through training. It is not just given to us. The training field can be things that we have chosen to do, but often it is the result of just living life in a fallen world, learning to navigate through life and keep our heads above water. Do we embrace the situations put before us with determination and focus and press through until we achieve the goal, and cross the finish line?

Enduring the Wilderness but Missing the Finish Line … Do Not Let "Fear" Stop You

Let us look at the story of the Israelites who were in Kadesh just outside of the Promise Land. They had traveled through the wilderness and were now looking into the land that God had promised the Israelites. They had almost completed the journey; the last step was to go in and take the land that God had already told them He would give them.

Read Numbers Chapter 13:1-3; 13:17 – Chapter 14:1-29.

What did God instruct Moses to do?

How long were the spies in Canaan?

What report did they bring back?

The Israelites made a fatal mistake. They forgot God's character. He had delivered them out of Egypt, protected them, fed them manna and quail, and fulfilled every promise He made to them. When God encouraged them through Moses to take the last step and enter the land, they refused to go. Why? After all, this had been their goal for years. What happened? FEAR gripped them. They stopped in their tracks. Worse yet, they wanted to turn around and run right back to Egypt where they had been enslaved.

Read the following Scriptures and answer the questions below:

Numbers 13:27-28:

> *"We went into the land which you sent us, and it does flow with milk and honey! Here is the fruit. But the people who live there are powerful, and the cities are fortified and very large. We even saw descendant of Anak there." (NIV)*

How did the spies describe the land?

What was Caleb's response to the Israelites?

Read Numbers 13:31-33.

What was their response?

Write a list of the words the spies used to describe the people in the promised land?

What do those words describe to you?

Then the people responded with weeping and crying all night. They even said that they wish they had died in Egypt rather than being where they were. The people began planning to return to Egypt. At this Moses and Aaron "fell face downward on the ground before the people of Israel." Joshua and Caleb (two of the spies) ripped their clothing and tried encouraging the Israelites. Their hearts were hardened. Fear filled them. The Israelites, God's chosen people, had given up.

Read Numbers 14:6-9.

What did Caleb and Joshua tell the Israelites?

What did Joshua and Caleb tell the Israelites twice in verse 9?

Joshua, Caleb and Moses tried to convince the people to look past their fear and believe what God had spoken to them. God will lead us and speak to us along the way, but He also expects us to listen and obey Him when he does.

Read Numbers 14:20-35. How did God react to the fear that consumed His people? Write down the words God spoke to the Israelites.

Put yourself in Moses' shoes. How do you think he felt?

How do you think God felt?

As I read this, I cannot help but wonder how God's voice sounded when He said this. We know from the paragraph to follow that God was angry. I wonder what you could hear in His voice. Did Moses hear the hurt and disbelief of God in His own chosen people not believing Him? After all He had done for them, freeing them from their slavery in Egypt, leading them through the desert, providing manna and quail and water for them. Did they forget the cloud that led them by day and the pillar of fire by night? What happened to their faith in Yahweh? Moses begged God to forgive them and to show His love by not destroying them. God relents and pardons them. But there are consequences for their sin and unbelief.

The spies were sent to the Promised Land to determine where to enter the Promise Land – not if they should enter. God had already said "go", but they were afraid of the risk and did not want to enter. They let fear and skepticism rule. God gives His people the power to overcome. If only they believed … if only they persevered until the very end! It only took 11 days to go from where the Israelites started in Egypt to the Promise Land. Instead, they ended up wandering around the wilderness for 40 years, one year for each day the spies had spent in Canaan seeing the goodness of the Lord. It was not the distance that stood between them and the Promised Land, but the condition of their hearts. When God tells me to break camp and move out to face a challenge which He gives me, will I obey? God takes seriously our grumbling, criticism, and contempt. He calls us to not give up, to persevere, to trust Him and not rely on our own emotions.

Day 2:
DO NOT LET DISOBEDIENCE TAKE YOUR DREAM!

Caleb and Joshua followed God with all their heart, and they were rewarded for their obedience and perseverance. Caleb and Joshua stood alone on the side of truth. They had faith in a great God, even when others did not. In Deuteronomy 1:29, we see Moses encouraging Joshua and Caleb with these words: "Do not be terrified; do not be afraid of them. The Lord your God is going before you and will fight for you." They pushed through and persevered, and they walked into the Promised Land.

Cinda stated two basic reasons we do not experience more perseverance in our own lives or see it displayed in those around us:

1. "Most individuals do not possess a vision for their lives that is greater than themselves."

2. "Perseverance usually emerges from the depths of a testing or trial, and we all hate those."[38]

The Israelites could not get past their own fear. It immobilized them from going in and taking the land that God already said He was giving to them. They did not focus on WHO said to go in. The God of the impossible was assuring them He was giving the land to them. Their vision did not go beyond their own self-preservation. We all seek self-preservation. It is natural. It is part of being human. But when God speaks a word, we need not fear. Our response should be obedience. This was not meant to be a test but ended up being one. Only Joshua and Caleb passed the test and later walked into the Promised Land. The rest of the men who refused to obey ended up wandering the desert till their eventual death.

Do I see God's glory and miraculous signs in my life, but still disobey and test Him?

Do I treat God with contempt when I do not trust Him?

Do not stop trusting God just as you are about to reach your goal. He brought you this far, and He will not let you down. Continue to trust Him, remembering His faithfulness over the past years of your life. (The fact that you are here doing this study, shows that He has been faithful!)

There have been times when I thought I was just about to meet my goal, and life took an unexpected turn leaving me feeling like someone had moved the finish line. The end somehow faded off into the distance again. What we do here determines if we persevere. Do we give up, or do we refocus and press forward once again, to accomplish the goal we had originally determined to attain?

So often life can look hopeless, but hope is right around the corner. You just cannot see it yet. God will always come through when you reject fear and persevere. Often when we do cross over the finish line, we can look behind us and see why things happened the way they did as we journeyed through life. Life events line up and build upon each other to bring you to this place where God wants to show you His faithfulness.

"Fearful" versus "Fearless"

The Christian life requires faith and hard work. To live effectively we must consistently keep our eyes on Jesus. We will stumble if we look away from Him and focus on the circumstances surrounding us. Peter, Jesus' disciple, had a habit of going from fearless and full of faith one moment to fearful and faithless the next. When his eyes waivered, so did his faith.

Read Matthew 14:22-33:

Who are the people in this story?

What difficult situation were the disciples in?

What did Peter ask the Lord?

Take special note of Matthew 14:30:

> "But when he saw the wind, he was afraid and beginning to sink, and cried out,
> "Lord, save me!" Immediately Jesus reached out his hand and caught him. "You of little faith,"
> he said, "Why did you doubt?" (NIV)

When did Peter start to sink?

What was Jesus' response to Peter's cry for help?

Why do you think Peter doubted?

Why do you doubt when there is a "storm" in your life?

Fear and Worry Go Hand in Hand

"Therefore, I tell you, do not be anxious about your life, what you will eat or what you will drink, nor about your body, what you will put on. Is not life more than food, and the body more than clothing? Look at the birds of the air: they neither sow nor reap nor gather into barns, and yet your heavenly Father feeds them. Are you not of more value than they? And which of you by being anxious can add a single hour to his span of life?" Matthew 6:25-27 (ESV)

What does Jesus tell us not to worry about?

What does He tell us to do?

Read the Scriptures below and write down what Jesus tells us to do instead of worry?

1 Peter 5:7

Isaiah 43:1-3

John 14:27

Worry can turn into fear in a matter of seconds, and fear is not from God. The thing you fear often never becomes reality. If it does, God will give you the grace for it when needed, not in advance. God always comes through in the long run. We like to be independent and prepared for anything, but He wants us to learn to trust Him and stand firm in our faith while passing through the storm. We are not to panic or become fearful, but He calls us to partner with Him, persevere, and see His faithfulness in our life. By endurance we show that our faith is real. It is the hope and faith in God that pushes us forward despite the difficulties and situations we find ourselves in.

Overcoming Fear to Do Great Things

Throughout the Bible we see many stories of how God approached an ordinary man and asked him to do difficult tasks. Most of their initial reactions were full-fledged fear. Moses tried to get out of it by saying he was not good at talking. Gideon was scared, so he tested God with a fleece, not once but twice. And then there was Saul hiding amongst baggage when he was to be announced as King.

Just like us, people in the Bible struggled. If we do not allow ourselves to get immobilized by fear, God can accomplish great things through us. Let us look at the disciples in their last hours with Jesus. These were the people who knew Jesus best. The disciples had lived with Jesus for three years and believed He was the Son of God. However, when their world was shaken, they ran. Jesus told the disciples they would run. Peter was the only one who said he would not (but he did). I am sure all of them thought they would stand firm by Jesus. But then the reality happened. They scattered. They ran away when Jesus was facing His most difficult hours.

Complete the blanks in the Scriptures below.

Mark 14:27

"You will all _____ away," Jesus told them, "for it is written "I will strike the shepherd and the sheep will be _____ ." (NIV)

Mark 14:50

"Then everyone _____ him and fled." (NIV)

Mark 14:51

"A young man, wearing nothing but a linen garment was following Jesus. When they seized him, he _____ naked, leaving his garment behind." (NIV)

Mark 14:72

"Immediately the rooster crowed the second time. Then Peter remembered the word Jesus had spoken to him. Before the rooster crows twice you will _____ me three times. And he broke down and wept." (NIV)

In confusion, fear and mourning, the disciples hid themselves behind closed doors. Jesus was crucified. Only John was at the crucifixion. The rest were nowhere to be found.

Fear has a way of gripping us in such a way that even when the "truth" is right in front of us our eyes can be blinded to it. Jesus' initial resurrected presence did not change their fear. It is when He spoke to them, that perfect love began casting out fear. He showed them proof, because the human mind often demands that, even though Jesus' presence should have been enough. Their fear was exchanged for joy in the presence of God.

> *"Jesus himself stood among them and said to them, "Peace be with you." They were startled and frightened, thinking they saw a ghost. He said to them "Why are you troubled, and why do doubts rise in your minds? Look at my hands and feet. It is I, myself! Touch me and see. A ghost does not have flesh and bones, as you see I have."" Luke 24:36-37 (NIV)*

Great Commission – The Disciples Sent Out

Jesus spent time with His disciples after His resurrection. He assured them that He was alive and showed them proof of it.

> *"After his suffering, he presented himself to them and gave many convincing proofs that he was alive. He appeared to them over a period of forty days and spoke about the Kingdom of God." Acts 1:3 (NIV)*

It was during these forty days together that Jesus spoke to his disciples, giving them His vision (the Great Commission in Matthew 28:18-20) for their future. Jesus clearly explained His vision for them. He was specific about what He wanted. (God speaks in specifics: how to build the ark, how to build the tabernacle, how to build the temple, how to offer sacrifices.) God will direct you when He gives you a vision.

Circle the key words in each Scripture below that describe parts of the vision Jesus spoke to His disciples.

> *"On the evening of that first day of the week, when the disciples were together, with the doors locked for fear of the Jewish leaders, Jesus came and stood among them and said, "Peace be*

with you!" After he said this, he showed them his hands and side. The disciples were overjoyed when they saw the Lord. Again, Jesus said "Peace be with you! As the Father has sent me, I am sending you" And with that he breathed on them and said, "Receive the Holy Spirit."" John 20:19 (NIV)

"Then the eleven disciples went to Galilee, to the mountain where Jesus had told them to do. When they saw Him, they worshiped Him; but some doubted. Then Jesus came to them and said, "All authority in heaven and on earth has been given to me. Therefore, go and make disciples of all nations, baptizing them in the name of the Father and of the Son and of the Holy Spirit, and teaching them to obey everything I have commanded you. And surely, I will be with you always to the very end of the age."" Matthew 28:16-20 (NIV)

"Whoever believes and is baptized will be saved, but whoever does not believe will be condemned. And these signs will accompany those who believe: In My name they will drive out demons; they will speak in new tongues; they will pick up snakes with their hands; and when they drink deadly poison, it will not hurt them at all; they will place their hands on sick people, and they will get well." Mark 16:16-18 (NIV)

"Then the disciples went out and preached everywhere and the Lord worked with them and confirmed His word by the signs that accompanied it." Mark 16:20 (NIV)

On Fire – No Longer Fearful but Fearless!

Jesus had spent forty days with the disciples, and it was time for Him to return to the Father in heaven. But there was one vital element of the vision that needed to be given to the disciples of Jesus for them to accomplish the mission Jesus was sending them out to do. The key to their success was the Holy Spirit.

"You are witnesses of these things. I am going to send you what my Father has promised; but stay in the city until you have been clothed with power from on high." Luke 24:48-49 (NIV)

"When the day of Pentecost came, they were all together in one place. Suddenly a sound like the blowing of a violent wind came from heaven and filled the whole house where they were sitting. They saw what seemed to be tongues of fire that separated and came to rest on each of them. All of them were filled with the Holy Spirit and began to speak in other tongues as the Spirit enabled them." Acts 2:1-4 (NIV)

After the Holy Spirit came upon them, they were changed forever. They were consumed with the vision – go and preach the gospel to all nations. They could not be contained; they were like a

wildfire that had been set. Peter was no longer hiding from the crowds in Jerusalem, he was in front of them preaching with passion:

> Peter replied, "Repent and be baptized, every one of you, in the name of Jesus Christ so that your sins will be forgiven. And you will receive the gift of the Holy Spirit. The promise is for you and your children and for all who are far off – for all who the Lord our God will call."
> With many other words he warned them; and he pleaded with them, "Save yourselves from this corrupt generation." Those who accepted his message were baptized, and about three thousand were added to their number that day." Acts 2:38-41 (NIV)

Everyone listening could not help but see the change in these ordinary men, who turned out not so ordinary. When the Holy Spirit comes to dwell within us things are never "ordinary" again. Being with Jesus changes us.

> "Utterly amazed, they asked, "Are not all these men who are speaking Galileans? Then how is it that each of us hears them in his own native language?"" Acts 2:7-8 (NIV)

> "When they saw the courage of Peter and John and realized that they were unschooled, ordinary men, they were astonished and they took note that these men had been with Jesus." Acts 4:13 (NIV)

> "With great power the apostles continued to testify to the resurrection of the Lord Jesus, and much grace was upon them all." Acts 4:33 (NIV)

Fear was gone. Power and authority took up residence where fear once resided. A new boldness had emerged; Jesus' vision for his disciples had been given and now it was being accomplished. The Church was being established wherever they went. People were hearing the gospel and becoming believers. The Church was explosively growing.

Read the following Scriptures and write down the changes that happened as they stepped out into what God had planned for them.

Acts 2:42-47

Acts 4:15-20

Acts 5:27-29

Acts 5:41

Acts 7:51

These meek, fearful men became bold proclaimers of the gospel. They traveled all around and preached the good news about Jesus. Regardless of the threats against them and the persecution and suffering they experienced, they never backed down from their message. Almost all the disciples died a martyr's death. The disciples were full of courage and did not let fear stop them from proclaiming the gospel message right up till their deaths.

God calls us to be fearless. In Matthew 28:20 Jesus said to His disciples, and to us, "Behold I am with you till the end of time." Our society is not much different from the disciple's society. Their message was accepted by many, but they were also mocked, rejected and persecuted for their faith. Many Christians around the world are experiencing the same thing, and they too, like the disciples, stand boldly and proclaim the gospel of Jesus. The Holy Spirit who dwells in us gives us our boldness, our courage to persevere. Without the Holy Spirit, many of us would be immobilized in our fear. The words "Be strong and courageous, for the Lord your God is with you," spoken in the Old Testament, still apply to us. When the power of the Holy Spirit dwells in you, you have nothing to fear. So be bold. Be courageous. Embrace your vision and fulfill it!

Day 3:
WAYS GOD ENCOURAGES US

We are not alone. Satan whispers, "No one cares, no one loves you, you are all alone." Yet the truth is there are angels that God sent to surround you to protect you (Psalms 91:11). Those who you loved who are in heaven right now are cheering you on as you journey through this life looking heavenward for the ultimate prize. Jesus himself tells us that He will never leave us or forsake us, He is with us and is interceding for us to the Father. God has given us fellow brothers and sisters in the faith, the Body of Christ, with whom we have fellowship; we have an army surrounding us making sure we finish strong!

> "Therefore, since we are surrounded by such a great cloud of witnesses, let us throw off everything that hinders and sin that so easily entangles. And let us run with perseverance the race marked out for us." Hebrews 12:1 (NIV)

God encourages us to persevere in many ways, but we will look at three specific ways God helps us to tenaciously run the race.

#1: God Has Given Us His Word to Guide Us

What do the following Scriptures say reading the Word of God can do for us?

Romans 15:4

John 8:32

John 17:17

2 Timothy 3:16

Hebrews 4:12

Scripture was written to be our guide. From Genesis to Revelation, God teaches us through peoples' examples of how to persevere. The Bible is full of examples of people that pressed through difficult life situations and did not give up until they obtained that which they were seeking. It is these Biblical examples that encourage our faith. If others are able to persevere through a difficult crisis or situation, it shows that it can be done. If they can do it, we can!

Thoughts to Ponder on not Giving up!

"The difference between success and failure is often simply perseverance." John Vickers[39]

"Many of life's failures are people who did not realize how close they were to success when they gave up." Thomas Edison[40]

"It's not that I'm smart, it's just that I stay with problems longer." Albert Einstein[41]

Perseverance is critical to running this race we call life. We all know people who have done this well, and maybe some who gave up too soon.

List the names of some of the people in your life that have encouraged you to persevere.

#2: The Holy Spirit Dwells Within Us and Empowers Us

"Don't you not know that you yourselves are God's temple and that God's Spirit lives in you. If anyone destroys God's temple, God will destroy him, for God's temple is sacred, and you are that temple." 1 Corinthians 3:16-17 (NIV)

"I have been crucified with Christ; and it is no longer I that live, but Christ lives in me." Galatians 2:20 (ESV)

Read the following Scriptures and list how God helps us.

2 Peter 1:2-9

Acts 1:8

John 14:26

Ezekiel 36:27

Luke 12:12

Ephesians 1:17

The moment you became a believer, the Holy Spirit came to dwell in you. He took up residence. He occupied you. It is His Spirit dwelling in us that sets us free. It is His Spirit in us that transforms us into the image of Christ. It is the Holy Spirit that empowers you to walk in the power and authority of God. When we begin to partner with the Holy Spirit, we will receive the power, grace and authority to walk in freedom.

 #3: God Gives Us Hope!

God is the giver of hope. We do not have to live in the past, it is over and done. Finished! Fertig! Terminado! Finito! We are not to look back but look to the future that is rich in hope. When we walk with God we are looking to the future. It is something that is yet to come.

> *"Now faith is being sure of what we hope for and certain of what we do not see."*
> *Hebrews 11:1 (NIV)*

Describe the characteristics of hope as spoken in the Scriptures below:

Romans 5:5

2 Corinthians 4:18

Hebrews 6:19

Hebrews 10:22

In the Old Testament hope meant "to wait in expectancy." God wants us to wait in hopeful expectancy because He has good things planned for us.

> *"For in this hope we are saved. But hope that is seen is no hope at all. Who hopes for what they already have? But if we hope for what we do not yet have, we wait patiently for it." Romans 8:24-25 (NIV)*

While we are waiting for that which we do not yet have, we are told that we are to "wait patiently." I do not know too many people that would say the word "wait" is their favorite word. Our society is not about waiting. We want things fast and immediate and if we feel even a minute is wasted, we often become irritated that the response is taking too long. In the Scriptures, we see that God uses the word "wait" quite often. It is in the waiting that we are changed. It is in the waiting we need perseverance. As Solomon said in the Book of Ecclesiastes 3:1-8, "There is a time for everything." God's timing is critical. It is in the fulfillment of God's time that the promises of God unfold in our life. He determined before you were born that you would be born on a specific day. He determined that you would meet your spouse at a certain time, that your children will be born according to His timetable, and even the day we leave this earth has been determined. God's timing throughout our life is critical. When we understand this concept of waiting through God's eyes, our life will be filled with a greater measure of peace.

Read the following Scriptures on waiting and fill in the blanks:

Genesis 18:14

"Is there anything too hard for the Lord? I will return to you at the _____ next year and Sarah will have a son." (NIV)

Psalm 27:14

"_____ for the Lord; be strong and take heart and _____ for the Lord." (NIV)

Psalm 37:7

"Be still before the Lord and _____ for him." (NIV)

Psalm 37:34

"_____ in the Lord and keep his _____ ." (NIV)

Ecclesiastes 3:1

"There is a _____ for everything, and a _____ for every activity under the heavens." (NIV)

Ecclesiastes 3:11

"He has made everything beautiful _____ . He has also _____ in the hearts of men; yet they cannot fathom what God has done from beginning to end." (NIV)

Psalm 40:1-2

"I _____ for the Lord; he turned to me and heard my cry. He lifted me out of the slimy pit out of the mud and mire." (NIV)

Isaiah 30:18

"The Lord longs to be gracious to you; he rises to show you compassion. For the Lord is a God of justice. _____ are all those who _____ for him." (NIV)

Galatians 4:4

"But when the _____ had _____ come..." (NIV)

Ephesians 1:10

"when _____ reach their _____ ." Eph 1:10 (NIV)

When we wait, whether patiently or not, we learn to persevere. It is in the waiting that God lines things up, gets things ready, changes our hearts or the hearts of others with whom we will be in contact. God is working during the waiting, sometimes on us, sometimes on others and sometimes on circumstances. One thing for sure is that He has a plan and when we persevere, we will be rewarded.

What do the following Scriptures say about perseverance?

James 1:2-4

James 5:11

Romans 5:3

1 Peter 4:12-13

James does not say "if" you face trials but "whenever" you face them. You will have trials, but you can also profit from them. James tells us to turn our hardships into times of learning. Trials can produce positive things for us if we let them. It is in the tough times that we develop perseverance. Even Jesus had to deal with persevering here on this earth.

> *"May the Lord direct your hearts into God's love and Christ's perseverance."*
> *2 Thessalonians 3:5 (NIV)*

What do you think "Christ's perseverance" means?

Jesus modeled perseverance continually. In His final days he experienced physical and emotional pain, yet He kept His eyes on the Father and on what the Father called Him to do. Jesus experienced emotional stress in a way we will never experience, in sweating blood. As Jesus pleaded with the Father in the Garden to take the cup of suffering away from Him (Luke 22:42 NLT) He experienced the feeling of dread. Jesus experienced physical pain from being struck, being whipped, to hanging on the cross and suffocating to death. Yet He persevered through all this trauma by keeping His eyes on the Father and His Father's will.

Read Romans 2:7-8:

> *"To those who by persistence in doing good seek glory, honor and immortality, He will give eternal life. But for those who are self-seeking and who reject the truth and follow evil, there will be wrath and anger." (NIV)*

What does persistence bring?

The crown of life is like the victory wreath given to winning athletes (1 Cor 9:25). God's crown of life is not glory and honor here on earth, but the reward of eternal life – living with God forever. The way to God's winning circle is by loving Him and staying faithful even under pressure. Persevering in this world and accomplishing the purpose with which He has entrusted us.

The apostle Paul tells us that in the future we will become like Jesus, but until then we must overcome. We will experience difficulties that help us grow. We rejoice in suffering not because we like pain or trauma, but because we know that God is using life's difficulties and Satan's attacks to build our character. The problems we run into will develop our perseverance which will strengthen our character and deepen our trust in God giving us greater confidence about the future. When we find our patience being tested, thank God for opportunities to grow and deal with problems using His strength and power. Paul assures us that those who patiently and persistently do God's will shall find eternal life. When we commit our lives fully to God, we want to please Him and do His will. As such, our good deeds are a grateful response to what God has done, not a prerequisite to earning His grace and salvation.

Day 4:
PROGRESSION TOWARD YOUR VISION IS A CHOICE

"Where there is no vision, the people perish." Proverbs 29:18 (KJV)

A person who has a vision, a goal that is bigger than themselves, will look at things differently than a person who is just going through life haphazardly. When trials come, they focus on that vision, keeping it as their foremost thought. With this mindset, everything is filtered through the lens of the vision and therefore influences their decisions and the actions in which they choose to take part.

In her book, Cinda states: "When faced with hardships or trials, it is very tempting to give up and lose hope if you do not have a specific purpose propelling you forward. It is human nature to desire personal comfort, thus avoiding all trials and tribulations becomes our focus."[42]

"Instead of pouring all our energy into trying to avoid or escape trials, we inwardly said "yes" to the process, knowing that as we embraced it, stronger character traits would develop, rendering us far more effective in our ministry. Our vision became our "true north." We realized that each choice mattered, and that God had instilled in us the potential to make a difference to all we met. If we choose to quit or become discouraged it would not only impact us, but also the many others we were called to help."[43]

The lens has changed. We are looking at the circumstances of our life through the lens of the "vision" God has given us. The key is, each time we face a trial or difficult decision, choose to move forward. Moving forward is a decision you will make over and over. A decision to keep on trying. A decision to not react in emotion, but in love. A decision to not worry about tomorrow. A decision to look beyond the circumstance of today to the plan which God is unfolding through the circumstances of this moment.

> *"And not only that, but we also glory in tribulations, knowing that tribulation produces perseverance; and perseverance, character; and character hope. Now hope does not disappoint, because the love of God has been poured out in our hearts by the Holy Spirit who was given to us." Romans 5:3-5 (RSV)*

Cinda goes on to explain how internalizing God's vision changed her and her husband. "Giving in and giving up were no longer options once we had internalized God's vision. Perseverance was the only rational course of action. Ever so slowly, God began to instill perseverance into our characters.

Each time we faced a trial, we would deliberately choose to progress toward our vision, to not give up, to not lose hope. The more we exercised perseverance, the more it became second nature. After a period of time, it became habit. Finally, it became part of our identities."[44]

God has given you the Holy Spirit! The Holy Spirit who dwells within you brings hope to any situation in which you find yourself. He will help you discern the evil spirits in the world and their schemes and deception. He knows the truth, and He will guide and direct your path by opening your eyes and ears to truth as you faithfully walk out your vision.

The Holy Spirit can also help guide us in what tools we should embrace in our growth process toward our vision. There are all kinds of tools that can facilitate growth: Bible studies on specific topics that relate to your call, conferences, seminars, books, mentors just to name a few. Meditate on God's Word. Study. Pray. Wait. Move.

It is critical to know our standing in the world if we are to move forward in our vision.

Read 1 John 4:4-6:

> "You, dear children, are from God and have overcome them, because the one who is in you is greater than the one who is in the world. The (evil spirits) are from the world and therefore speak from the viewpoint of the world, and the world listens to them. We are from God, and whoever knows God listens to us; but whoever is not from God does not listen to us. This is how we recognize the Spirit of truth and the spirit of falsehood." (NIV)

What have we "overcome"?

What allows us to be "overcomers"?

How do we discern evil spirits and the schemes of Satan?

You have a great source of power and strength at your disposal: The Holy Spirit lives in you. Together you can go through anything because His power is stronger than any circumstance. Hope dwells within you, so embrace it. As you partner together with God, you will persevere.

Day 5:
STANDING FIRM

Standing firm takes strength. To be firm one is "unmovable". There are many people in the Bible that displayed this type of strength. When David faced Goliath, his faith in God was stronger than his fear, and God delivered Goliath into David's hand with a sling and a stone. Daniel never stopped praying and worshipping the Lord even though it was against the law. He would not compromise his belief in God. He was thrown into the lion's den, and the hungry lions ignored him. Shadrack, Meshack and Abednego would not bow down to the golden statue and worship. They stood firm in their faith and refused to worship anyone or anything except Yahweh. They were thrown into the fiery furnace. They not only did not die, but God sent them a companion in the furnace. When they came out, their circumstance had not even affected them – they did not even smell like smoke!

The disciples stood firm in their faith and placed their hope in God regardless of the threats that stood against them. They were unwavering; how about us? Do we stand firm in the midst of trials? God is calling us to stand firm, to keep our eyes on Him rather than the storms around us. Remember Peter when he walked on the water? He only began to sink when his eyes went from looking at Jesus to the waves and storm that surrounded him. Stand firm, and watch God show up.

Standing firm will take perseverance because our faith will be challenged and opposed. Enduring to the end does not earn salvation for us but shows the power of being saved. The assurance of our salvation will keep us going through times of persecution and suffering.

Read the following Scriptures about standing firm and answer the questions below each one.

> *"It is for freedom that Christ has set us free! Stand firm, then, and do not let yourselves be burdened again by a yoke of slavery." Galatians 5:1 (NIV)*

What do we not allow by standing firm?

God does not ask us to stand firm without giving us the tools to stand firm. He tells us how we can stand firm and what we need to do it.

Read Ephesians 6:13-17:

"Therefore, put on the full armor of God, so when the day of evil comes, you may be able to stand your ground, and after you have done everything, to stand. Stand firm then, with the belt of truth buckled around your waist, with the breastplate of righteousness in place, and with your feet fitted with the readiness that comes from the gospel of peace. In addition to all this, take up the shield of faith, with which you can extinguish all the flaming arrows of the evil one. Take the helmet of salvation and the sword of the Spirit, which is the word of God." (NIV)

To stand our ground and stand firm we need to be dressed in the armor of God. List each piece of armor and what it represents.

How does your armor look? Are there any chinks in your armor? What areas do you need to work on?

Not only do we have the armor of God that will help us stand firm, but we are also given the Body of Christ to help us. Paul in his writing to the Philippian church told them they will stand firm when they stand together.

"Whatever happens, conduct yourselves in a manner worthy of the gospel of Christ. Then, whether I come to see you or only hear about you in my absence, I will know that you stand firm in the one Spirit, striving together as one for the faith of the gospel without being frightened in any way by those who oppose you." Philippians 1:27-28a (NIV)

In what do we stand firm?

Learning how to persevere is critical to enable us to navigate tumultuous times ahead. If we have not learned to persevere and keep our eyes focused on Jesus, we are in danger.

"Then you will be handed over to be persecuted and put to death, and you will be hated by all nations because of me. At that time many will turn away from the faith and will betray and hate each other, and many false prophets will appear and deceive many people. Because of the increase of wickedness, the love of most will grow cold, but he who stands firm to the end will be saved." Matthew 24:9-13 (NIV)

What warning do you see here?

What encouragement does it give to those who stand firm?

What are some things you can do to protect yourself from your love growing cold?

We are told that God at the end of time is going to separate the people here on earth (Matthew 13:49 and Matthew 25:31-33). Trials bring what is in us to the surface and sifts out true Christians from false or fair-weather Christians. When you are pressured to give up and turn your back on Christ, do not do it. It takes work, focus and perseverance to stay on the right path. Remember the benefits of when you stand firm and continue to live for the Lord.

Sometimes life can look hopeless, but the reality is hope is right around the corner. We often just cannot see it. God always comes through. Sometimes things only make sense when we look backwards and see what God has done.

Do not panic in the short term, for God will work it out in the long run. The thing you fear that is coming is not actually here yet and there is a good chance it will not happen. When and if it arrives, God will give you the grace for it when needed, not in advance. Take heart, God always comes through in the long run. We like to be independent and prepared for whatever may come, but He wants us to learn to trust Him and stand firm in our faith while passing through the storms and trials this world brings.

Read the Scriptures below and write down the keys to walking in perseverance:

Proverbs 3:5-6

James 1:4

Romans 5:3

We persevere because it has an important outcome. Trusting the Lord, regardless if we understand why things are happening, is foundational to persevering. When you persevere through the trials

and difficult times, you gain something you would not have if you did not push through: you become mature and complete in your faith. We often learn best when we are pushed to be our best.

When we walk in trust and faith, we will discover that it is much easier to persevere, because we know that God has already worked out things for us and that God is always going to do what is best for us. So, we can persevere and wait patiently for God to direct us in our next step. Do not run ahead of him. Wait for Him to lead you through any storms that you experience in this life.

> *"Therefore, my dear friends, as you have always obeyed – not only in my presence, but now much more in my absence - continue to work out your salvation with fear and trembling, for it is God who works in you to will and to act in order to fulfill his good purpose. Do everything without grumbling or arguing, so that you may become blameless and pure, "children of God without fault in a warped and crooked generation." Then you will shine among them like stars in the sky as you hold firmly to the word of life." Philippians 2:12-16a (NIV)*

Those who persevere through the sufferings and trials this life gives will look different to the world. Your hope will shine like the stars for all to see, and people will want to know where that hope comes from. So "shine like the stars" as you run the race toward the finish line and may all who know you cross the line with you.

Prayer for Choosing to Persevere and Not Give Up
by Cinda Gregory

"Heavenly Father, I come to You, realizing that Your ways are not always our ways…You always have our best interest and character in mind, whereas we sometimes are willing to sacrifice that to "find the easy way out." That attitude does not benefit anyone; not me, and not anyone around me. Perhaps the real issue is that I am reluctant to truly trust You with my life and future…Father, I repent for that attitude; I ask for your forgiveness. I want to make a difference in this world, and I know that is Your heart for me as well. Today I choose to wholly yield myself to You. Is there anything You would like to speak to my heart, Father?

God, would you speak to me afresh and share Your heart and dreams with me concerning my destiny? Would You speak to me in a special and unique way? I want to know the specific purpose and mandate that You have reserved for me as my own adventure. What have You specifically created me to do, Father? I want to partner with You; I want to be instrumental in bringing heaven down to earth! I want to make a difference! Share that vision with me, Father, and ignite the fire within.

I realize that nothing worthwhile is ever accomplished without perseverance. Father, although I may never have prayed a prayer like this before, I choose to trust You and ask You to build perseverance in my character. I know I can trust You. You love me more than I love myself, and I know I can trust You to choose what is best for me. I want my life to matter; I want to make a difference in the world. I want to have the character of Jesus. I yield my life to You. Let my life bring glory and honor to You!

I also realize that truly great feats require the effort of more than one solitary person. You have put us in "community" for a reason…We need each other. Father, if there are still areas of woundedness in my heart that have kept me from functioning effectively within the community You have placed me in, I ask your forgiveness. You know my heart, God. You know whether I have been harboring offenses; wearing a mask to protect myself so as to not be vulnerable and transparent. You know, Father, and so do I. I repent for any and all areas which I have not been honoring the blessing of community, and especially the community of family and church. I repent, I choose to turn from the way I have previously behaved and go in a new direction, the direction of your choosing.

I want to be a person that infectiously spreads LIFE and HOPE everywhere I go! I want to walk in new depths of life, hope, and faith. I know that is Your heart for me as well, so I ask that You take me by the hand and guide me into the deep waters. I choose to leave the shore of hum-drum safety and trust You in the adventures of this lifetime! I want to be a world changer, God, and I know that if I partner with You, it is guaranteed! Each day I choose to partner with You! I love You, Daddy." [45]

Final Thoughts

Most of us have some regrets about our past, but as you have studied, God is all about leaving the past behind, and so should you. Scripture tells us that life is like a mist or vapor (James 4:14). There are no guarantees for tomorrow. Only God holds the book of life. He knew your beginning, and He knows the day you will draw your last breath. From the beginning he carefully designed you with a purpose in mind. He created you with everything you need to accomplish His plan. Your goal is to keep your eyes on God and be the clay in the potter's hand. Allow the Father to mold and stretch you as you journey through this life so you can accomplish all He has planned for you. God has a great adventure for you. When Jesus became your Lord and Savior, the Holy Spirit came to dwell inside of you. At that moment, the plan and purposes of God became a reality for you. You are now able to walk in the "supernatural" things of God because the "supernatural" lives in you. God makes the impossible things possible. To accomplish His plan and purpose, He will give you authority to move in ways that you never dreamed. He will pour out His anointing on you so you can achieve what He desires. He will give you strength and power to be an "overcomer." God will give you a peace that surpasses all understanding when the storms of life crash like waves over you. He is the anchor that keeps you steady and holds you tight. Living a life with no regrets can be your reality.

🔑 **Key 1: Freedom-Our Choice to Be Whole** – Because God dwells within you, freedom is possible. The chains the enemy has wrapped around you can and will fall off when you believe that God has destined you to be free of your past and any strongholds that bind you. The Father went through tremendous pain to reclaim your freedom. He already fought the battle for you. Acknowledge the battle is over; you do not need to fight it. It is time to let God walk you through the process of reclaiming your freedom.

The first step to receiving freedom is believing that God wants you free. Bathe yourself in God's Word and let it speak truth and life over you. The Father makes it clear in His Word - freedom is yours. Allow yourself to go to those places of hurt, shame, guilt, and pain. Step into the place of vulnerability and transparency and pour out your heart and feelings to the Father. Give Him permission to take all the pieces — surrender it all to Him. Now let the Father speak truth over you and your situation. Often God may speak a single word (or words) into your mind or you may feel a sensation, you may see a picture or vision. If you sense God speaking to you, thank Him for what He has shown you or spoken to you. Receive it as His word over you. If you do not see or hear anything, thank God for taking all your pieces and for walking you into freedom. If you do not sense it immediately, it will come — God has promised you this. God has one focus for you — the future.

As Cinda stated in her book: "His desire to see us walk in freedom transcends our limited understanding. A very wise man once offered me a bit of advice I will always treasure… 'Heal your past; you'll redeem your future.' I am living proof of that!"[46]

Key 2: Choosing to Act in Love – The Bible has a lot to say about "love" and what true love looks like. When Jesus walked the earth, His desire was for people to experience the heart of the Father. It was through His love, which He expressed in words and actions, that drew the people to Him.

When talking to the Pharisees, Jesus stated that the most important commandment is to love the Lord your God, and secondly "You shall love your neighbor as yourself." Matthew 22:37-39 (NIV) He also said, "This is my **commandment,** that you love one another as I have loved you." John 15:12 (NKJV) It is all about love. When you love God first with your whole heart, you are then able to love your neighbor through your words and actions. God makes it clear what He wants you to do. You have the free will to decide. Will you choose to act in love regardless of how you feel? Jesus loved by serving. You are called to love in the same way.

It is through "loving" that people are changed. When people love, others will feel it. Cinda stated, "Choosing to walk in love has resulted in consistency and stability even when faced with a challenging season. I have learned not to only follow my emotions, as I then become easily offended. Instead, I do what I know to be right and show the person love, even when it is the opposite of what I feel like doing."[47] She also stated: "Love in action is a reflection of God's heart, and the rewards are great. I never require people to love me in return."[48] We cannot control other people's feelings toward us. That is why it is important to keep our focus on what God requires of us – to love regardless of how people treat us. Choose to love. Humble yourself, wrap the towel around your waist and begin to love and serve others. Loving others will bear much fruit in your life and bring glory to the Kingdom of God. "Faith, hope, and love. But the greatest of these is love." 1 Corinthians 13:13 (NIV)

Maya Angelou made the statement, "At the end of the day people won't remember what you said or did, they will remember how you made them feel."[49]

Key 3: Choosing to Be Vulnerable – The challenge set before you in week three was: are you willing to remove the masks you wear and become more transparent and vulnerable? Before you can let your guard down with others, you need to begin by letting your guard down with God. There are times when it is difficult to admit to God our true feelings, especially when you realize it may be God with whom you are offended. How you feel is no surprise to God. He already knows. The Father is waiting for you to be transparent and pour out your heart to Him. He will help you work through those things that you are going through. Transparency and vulnerability before God opens the door for Him to move. In the act of humbling and surrendering yourself to God's plan,

you are positioned into the place where God can begin to move the mountains in your life. If you hide from God, little change can happen. Invite God to come into those hidden places. He is trustworthy. God will meet you where you are. When you step out and remove your masks, all things are possible. Being vulnerable and transparent with God will bring a sense of relief and freedom. Often after being honest with your feelings, you can literally feel the chains fall off and a lightness enter your spirit. In the place of vulnerability and transparency, God can speak His truth into you and bring complete healing to your life.

Once you experience the freedom that vulnerability and transparency brings into your relationships and situations in your life, you will be able to use it to minister to others. When you speak honestly and openly from the heart, people will see how God has moved in your life, and they can experience hope for their situation. There are times you will share in more general terms. Other times God will ask you to go deeper and share details of something you went through. Let God guide you. In her book, Cinda said this about vulnerability: "My relationships are my most valued possessions. Whereas I use to strive to develop meaningful relationships, they now come naturally and easily. Vulnerability and transparency have been huge factors in this. It enables me to get to know people very quickly and to develop deep friendships with them because there are no walls between us."[50] Bob and Cinda made tremendous impact on my life by sharing situations they went through together. As they shared from the heart, they were raw and honest about the places they were in and how God stepped in and gave them victory. It was then I believed that if God helped them, He would help me. God uses vulnerability and transparency to bring down walls we have built.

Key 4: Intentional Growth Is a Choice – From the beginning of time, God has been intentional. God desires for you to be intentional. Often, too much is left to chance. If you do not plan, set goals to grow and develop, or even take time to think about what direction your life is taking, life will just happen to you. You will be like the wind, going this way and that, without any real purpose or direction. God does not want you to live like that. By living intentionally, you can fulfill the vision and plan God created you for. The key to living intentionally is spending time in the presence of God daily. It is in the quiet, alone time with God, that He can speak to us his strategic plan for the day, weeks, and months to come. The two most common ways God speaks is through His Word and prayer. When you find uninterrupted time with the Father, He can download His heart and His direction for you for that day.

Once God has spoken to you where He is leading you (the purpose He created you for), you should begin a growth plan. A growth plan will help you focus specifically on those things to which you believe God is calling you to. Growing and developing often requires you to invest in materials (books, DVD's, pod casts) or to attend conferences that focus on the vision or call that God has

given to you. As you fuel the fire of your passion for what God is calling you to, every investment you make toward your vision will pay off as you step out into your vision.

Always be ready for God to interrupt your plans. God uses people and circumstances to direct our path and lead us in the direction He wants us to go. Divine appointments, set up by God, are always God directing you to be a part of what He is already doing. There is no greater joy than walking in the destiny and purpose that God created you for! Start being intentional with your time and watch how God will walk you into the very purpose He created you for!

🗝 **Key 5: Partnering With God Is a Choice** – God has given you many tools in His Word to help you on your journey as a parent (if you do not have children, the same tools apply to other relationships you have in your life). When you rely completely on God with all your parenting issues, He will direct your path. You will make mistakes, but with God directing you, you can be a successful parent. The key to parenting is surrendering your children daily to the Father. When you place your loved ones at the feet of Jesus, you are entrusting them to God, believing that God has heard the cries of your heart and your prayers, and He will act according to His perfect will.

As a parent you raise your children to the best of your ability, but ultimately what they do is their choice, not yours. It is not a reflection on who you are. Take your stance in the Kingdom, standing firm in the knowledge that you are a beloved child of God. Regardless of what your children choose to do, you are not a failure in God's eyes. Continue trusting God and believing that God is good. God is your faithful partner, and He will guide and direct you as you parent. Never give up praying. Be your child's encourager and cheer them on when life is difficult. Stay on the watch tower and warn, guide, and direct in love if they will listen; otherwise just love them and pray. Continue to display unconditional love, even when it is costly or it seems like nothing is happening. Consistent, gentle, forgiving, unconditional love will move mountains. Believe in God's faithfulness.

🗝 **Key 6: Progression Toward Your Vision Is a Choice** – Too many people give up before they reach the finish line. They start the race strong, but do not finish well. In week six we studied the importance of keeping our eyes focused on the finish line. Persevering takes back bone. To persevere you must determine you are going to push through to the victory. God loves victory. He has fought battles that we could never fight so that you can be victorious. God tells you that you will have battles, struggles, and trials on earth, but you will ultimately be victorious if you keep your eyes on Jesus. This life is not the prize. Eternity with God is the prize. His presence in your life is what will carry you through the trials and suffering. God has made a promise to you; He is with you every step and will never leave you. When there is nothing this earth can give to comfort you or help you, God can. You must not forget that the very God you worship and love, lives inside of

you. So, wherever you go, He goes. Whatever you experience, He experiences. Whatever you feel, He feels. God knows firsthand what you are going through, and He is there to walk through the fire with you. The Holy Spirit will speak to you and give you direction, guidance, and strength for the journey. Do not neglect Him. God tells us that "in our weakness He is strong." When the Holy Spirit dwells within you, He will give you the strength and power to overcome anything. Keep your eyes and mind focused on Him. He will run beside you, and when you fall, He will pick you up and carry you to the finish line. God is your coach, your companion, and your inspiration – run the race to completion. Do not give up.

Perseverance teaches us who God is. He is a God that never gives up, never grows tired or weary and His knowledge, understanding and wisdom are far beyond our comprehension. God makes it clear that we do not think like Him. When the battle is real, the struggle exhausting and the pain is endless, keep your eyes focused on Him and trust in the fact that:

> *"For my thoughts are not your thoughts, neither are your ways my ways," declares the Lord. As the heavens are higher than the earth, so are my ways higher than your ways and my thoughts than your thoughts." Isaiah 55:8-9 (NIV)*

We are not going to understand God's thoughts or His ways completely. This verse is very comforting for it reminds us that He knows the better way. It is our job to believe that although we may not understand why things are happening the way they are, God knows, and He is in it and using it for our own good. Victory is closer than we think. When you persevere, you will often sense God's presence in ways you never have before. God is faithful. He will always show up for you. His strength is your strength. Call on Him to give you the strength to persevere when the enemy throws trials at you. When you gaze at Jesus, He fills you with hope that you can rise above the things of this world.

> *"To whom will you compare me? Or who is my equal?" says the Holy One. Lift your eyes and look to the heavens: Who created all these? He who brings out the starry host one by one and calls them each by name. Because of his great power and mighty strength, not one of them is missing. Why do you say, O Jacob, and complain, O Israel? My way is hidden from the Lord; my cause is disregarded by my God"? Do you not know? Have you not heard? The Lord is the everlasting God, the Creator of the ends of the earth. He will not grow tired or weary, and his understanding no one can fathom. He gives strength to the weary and increases the power of the weak. Even youths grow tired and weary, and young men stumble and fall; but those who hope in the Lord will renew their strength. They will soar on wings like eagles; they will run and not grow weary; they will walk and not be faint." Isaiah 40:25-31 (NIV)*

It is when you put your complete trust in God and believe Him at His Word that you will rise up. It is because of this hope you have in the Lord, that you can persevere. God promises the victory has been won, and you are victorious. You are an overcomer because of God's strength and His great love.

Do You Believe God?

"As the rain and the snow come down from heaven, and do not return to it without watering the earth and making it bud and flourish, so that it yields seed for the sower and bread for the eater, so is my word that goes out from my mouth; it will not return to me empty but will accomplish what I desire and achieve the purpose for which I sent it." Isaiah 55:10-11 (NIV)

God fully intends to keep His Word and promises that He has spoken to you. He gave you His promises so you can know what to believe. His promises and Word give you the foundation for what truth is. Stand confidently in the truth of God's Word. Everything hinges on what you believe.

"Not everyone that saith unto me, Lord, Lord, shall enter into the kingdom of heaven; but he who doeth the will of my Father which is in heaven." Matthew 7:21 (KJV)

What you do cannot be separated from what you believe. When you trust God and embrace His Word as truth, freedom cannot help but come because God says that He came to set the captive free. In Christ, freedom is yours. Your past is wiped out … it has no hold on you. God says that you are a new creation. God says that you are His beloved. God created you for a purpose. God says He is your healer. God says He will turn all things for the good, for those who love Him. God tells you He will direct your path and give you strength for the journey. He promises to restore your weary soul. There are so many promises … they are all for you. Believe them, apply them to your life, and "the truth shall set you free." To live a life without regrets you must learn to walk in the truth of His promises. Study His Word and let His truth sink into the depths of your soul. Receive the love He has for you. From the beginning of time, you were in His heart. The Good Shepherd has you in His arms. You are safe and secure.

"He tends his flock like a shepherd: He gathers the lambs in his arms and carries them close to his heart." Isaiah 40:11 (NIV)

You can trust Him completely. He will never fail you nor desert you. Rest in the Shepherd's arms and let Him lavish you with His love and restore your soul. You are His beloved child. You are His cherished creation. Walk in the fullness of His love for you, and you will never live with regret again.

Endnotes

Introduction

1   Cinda M. Gregory, <u>Living Without Regrets – 6 Essential Keys to Freedom,</u> ©2019, page 10

2   Dion Todd, Wasting Away, www.refreshinghope.org, June 22, 2021, Refreshing Hope Ministries, PO Box 67, Conway, SC 29528

Week 1: Freedom to Be Made Whole

3   Cinda M. Gregory, <u>Living Without Regrets – 6 Essential Keys to Freedom</u>, ©2019, page 7

4   ibid, page 10

5   Dion Todd, Journey of a Packhorse, <u>www.refreshinghope.org</u>, May 29, 2021, Refreshing Hope Ministries, PO Box 67, Conway SC 29528

6   ibid

7   Cinda M. Gregory, <u>Living Without Regrets – 6 Essential Keys to Freedom</u>, ©2019, page 13

8   Beth Moore, <u>It's Tough Being a Woman</u>, Lifeway Press, Nashville, TN 2008

9   Cinda M Gregory, <u>Living Without Regrets – 6 Essential Keys to Freedom</u>, page 15

10 ibid, Prayer for Choosing Freedom, pages 17-18

Week 2: Love Is More Than an Emotion

11 Heidi Baker, "Love Must Look like Something", IRIS Ministries, YouTube, 5/02/2013

12 Cinda M. Gregory, <u>Living Without Regrets – 6 Essential Keys to Freedom</u>, ©2019, page 19

13 ibid, page 25

14 ibid, page 32

15 ibid, page 27

16 Todd White, "Just Be Jesus – Just Be Love", Firestorm Conference, Lancaster, PA

17 Cinda M. Gregory, <u>Living Without Regrets – 6 Essential Keys to Freedom</u>, Prayer for Choosing to Love, ©2019, pages 38-39

Week 3: Removing the Mask

18 Merriam Webster Dictionary, www.merriam-webster.com

19 ibid

20 Cinda M. Gregory, <u>Living Without Regrets – 6 Essential Keys to Freedom</u>, ©2019, page 46

21 ibid, page 47

22 Beth Moore, <u>Here and Now…There and Then – A Lecture Series on Revelation</u>, ©2009, Living Proof Ministries, PO Box 84049, Houston, Texas, BETHMOORE.ORG

23 Cinda M. Gregory, <u>Living Without Regrets – 6 Essential Keys to Freedom</u>, Prayer for Choosing to Remove the Mask ©2019, pages 63-64

Week 4: Leaving Chance Behind

24 Joanna Gaines, Magnolia Journal, Issue no. 6 (Spring 2018), Intentional Living, Meredith Corporation

25 John Maxwell, <u>Intentional Living: Choosing a Life That Matters</u>, www.goodreads.com/work/quotes/44461012

26 Sarah Young, <u>Jesus Calling</u>, Thomas Nelson, Inc., Nashville, TN, Copyright 2004

27 James Strong, <u>The New Strong's Expanded Exhaustive Concordance of the Bible</u>, Thomas Nelson Publishers, Nashville, TN, ©2004

28 John Maxwell, Leadership Conference, Syracuse, New York

29 Cinda M Gregory, <u>Living Without Regrets – 6 Essential Keys to Freedom</u>, Prayer for Choosing to Be Intentional, ©2019, pages 75-76

Week 5: Parenting Without an Identity Crisis

30 Elizabeth Stone, The Village Voice, https//www.quoteswave.com/authors/Elizabeth-Stone

31 Barbara Johnson, <u>Splashes of Joy In the Cesspools of Life</u>, Word Publishing, ©1992, pages 59-61

32 Cinda M. Gregory, <u>Living Without Regrets – 6 Essential Keys to Freedom</u>, ©2019, page 80

33 ibid, page 83

34 ibid, page 84

35 ibid, Prayer for Choosing to Parent Without an Identity Crisis, page 84

Week 6: Perseverance

36 www.goodreads.com/author/quotes, Thomas Edison

37 Merriam Webster Dictionary online, www.merriam-webster.com

38 Cinda M. Gregory, <u>Living Without Regrets – 6 Essential Keys to Freedom</u>, ©2019, page 98

39 Linkedin.com, John Vickers, April 30, 2016

40 Brainy Quote.com, Thomas Edison

41 BrainyQuote.com, Albert Einstein

42 Cinda M. Gregory, <u>Living Without Regrets – 6 Essential Keys to Freedom</u>, ©2019, page 101

43 ibid page 102

44 ibid page 103

45 ibid, Prayer for Choosing to Persevere and Not Give Up, pages 115-116

Final Thoughts

46 Cinda M. Gregory, <u>Living Without Regrets – 6 Essential Keys to Freedom</u>, ©2019, page 16

47 ibid, page 36

48 ibid, page 37

49 www.goodreads.com/author/quotes, Maya Angelou

50 Cinda M. Gregory, <u>Living Without Regrets – 6 Essential Keys to Freedom</u>, ©2019, page 62